Echoes of Epping Forest

Oral History
of the
20th Century Forest

The Corporation of London

ISBN 085 203 084 3

Published by the Corporation of London
2004

Further copies are available from the Epping Forest
Information Centre, High Beach, Loughton, Essex
IG10 4AF

Printed in Great Britain by Riverside Press,
Ipswich IP2 8JX

Preface

The twentieth century certainly did not bypass Epping Forest. The Forest may have existed here for thousands of years and seem timeless to us but it was affected by the Second World War, urban development and social changes as much as any other part of the country.

The Forest has provided a unifying experience for many local people. "The Forest was our playground" has been a common phrase during this project and the Forest has provided basic living requirements such as firewood and food but also adventures, lifelong hobbies and a place for tranquillity and reflection. So many of these memories are of a similar character but are totally unique to the individual.

The Echoes of Epping Forest oral history project took place over 18 months. Almost 60 people contributed, either by responding to appeals for information or by being invited to participate. Some were happy to be recorded on tape, others preferred to write down their memories. Those who spoke to our interviewers, John Hart, Christine Dyer and Chris Johnson (who interviewed Ken Hoy), mostly did so in a natural conversation with the interviewers, some used prompt notes and only a couple preferred to have a script in front of them. During editing certain words and phrases have been changed, omitted or added in an attempt to improve the readability of the stories but the character of the interviewee and the desired tone and meaning of the words spoken have always been retained.

Only extracts from the interviews or letters are included in this booklet. I do apologise to the interviewees that I have not been able to include more of each interview in this booklet. I had not appreciated at the start of this project how many responses we would get to our appeals for memories. The recordings of the full interviews with the interviewees' permission, as well as the letters will be placed in the Corporation of London's Archives.

Any oral history project is going to include factual errors, I have attempted to correct as many as I can but please forgive any which remain. Another possible failing of this booklet is that certain themes or people who might be considered key to a recent history of Epping Forest are omitted; this is not from a decision on my behalf but simply that none of our interviewees mentioned the event, theme or person. The project attempted to provide a snapshot of the Forest's recent past

I would like to thank John and Christine for their enthusiasm for this project, the time they freely devoted and the understanding that they brought to their interviews. I know that they will join me in saying that the greatest acknowledgement we have to make is of course to the contributors, whose willingness to discuss their love of the Forest has greatly enhanced our knowledge and appreciation of it. We hope that you will feel this way too.

Contributors

The Conservators of Epping Forest would like to thank the following people for their involvement in this project:

Ivy Alexander (neé Hicks), b.1924
Hilda Anslow, b.1915
Mary Ashbridge-Taylor, b. 1928
Walter Barber, b 1916
Harry Berry, b. 1911
John Besent, b.1944
Ron Bond, b. 1936
Harry Bitten, b.1924
Allan Brafield, b. 1918
Jean Brazier (nee Adams), b. 1929
Brain Brenchley, b.1939
Joyce Casey (neé Goldsmith), b. 1926
Tania Collins (neé Wess), b. 1944
Michael Davis, b. 1928
Roy Delaney, b.1931
Eric Dormer, b. 1921
Brian Dyer, b.1937
Herbert (Bill) Embling, b.1912
John (Jack) Farmer, b. 1911
Richard Fitch, b. 1944
Peter Fitch, b. 1933
Gordon Forster, b.1928
Stan Gailer, b.1925
David Gannicott, b. 1934
Frank Gentry, b. 1921
John Harvey, b.1920
Constance Hoe (neé Lam), b. 1922 and Lesley Hoe, b 1919
Kathleen Hollis (neé Buck), b.1930
Keith Howes, b. 1927
Ken Hoy, b. 1924
Alan Hughes, b.1926 d. 2004

Elizabeth Hughes (neé Collie), b 1922
Patricia Laver (neé Hardcastle), b.1940
Alexander Longmoor, b.1932
Beryl King, b. 1920
Eric Marwood, b. 1937
Sylvia Mason (neé Benford), b.1938
Irene MacIntosh (neé Trussler), b. 1927
Barbara Morris (neé Bartlett), b. 1927
Paul Moxey, b 1938
Irene Poole, (neé Rusling) b. 1922
Graham Rawlings, b. 1939
Peter Reeve, b.1936
Peter Read, b. 1943
Alan Sibley, b 1925
Alan Stewart, b. 1916
Marna Snook (neé Walker), b.1954
Jim Tilley, b. 1927
Jane White (neé Gray), b. 1923
Alf Wright, 1928

Interviewers:
Christine Dyer, John Hart, Chris Johnson, Rachael Holtom.

Typists:
Ann Youd, Jackie Nightingill

Picture Acknowledgements

All images are from the Corporation of London apart from the following:

Page 11	Barbara Morris	Page 55	Alan Stewart
Page 19	Beryl King	Page 68	Peter Read
Page 28	Elizabeth Hughes	Page 90	Loughton Gazette
Page 46	Ron Bond	Page 101	M Collins.
Page 50	Jane White	Page 105	Ron Bond
Page 53	Alan Stewart		

The front cover shows Forest Keepers Albert Holland, Edward Weedon and Dave Cheatle in 1974

Echoes of Epping Forest

Oral History of the 20th Century Forest

Contents

Chapter One - Childhood Playground

The majority of the twentieth century children who lived in and around Epping Forest treated the Forest as their "backyard" or "playground". Local youngsters used the Forest, as generations of people had done in the past, to collect fuel and food as well as for enjoyment and exercise. Patricia Laver remembers these more innocent days very clearly:

I was born in Theydon Bois in 1940. After the War when industry was getting onto its feet my father got a job working two weeks on and two weeks off. He was based in Edinburgh. After two weeks working he would get a coach from Edinburgh to Wakes Arms. He would 'phone us as he arrived there and that was my set off point to meet him half way. Imagine letting a six year old girl does this walk today!

For Kathleen Hollis the Forest was at the centre of her childhood:

My sisters and I spent many happy days of our childhood in Epping Forest. Our garden gate in Princes Road opened on the Forest, Lords Bushes and Knighton Woods. We knew every pathway like a map. Many places had names- Side Path, Middle Path, Sutton's Bump, the Jungle and the Plain. We enjoyed going wooding with my mother to get wood. We were only allowed the dead wood to help boil our copper, to get hot water for washing and bath night. In the autumn we piled leaves in heaps to jump into from trees, or if we were lucky enough to find an old pram, we had a race track.

Whilst Hilda Anslow can recall the tastes of the Forest very vividly:

At the back of Strawberry Hill Pond there was a cluster of sweet chestnut trees, and we usually collected several bags of fair sized chestnuts each year. I don't know whether it was our imagination but they tasted much better than bought ones. The crab apples also seemed much bigger then and it didn't take long to pick up enough to make several jars of crab apple jelly.

For some little boys, the Forest provided endless days of adventures,

and to fuel their escapades they illegally plundered the Forest, producing the strangest of meals. Peter Read remembers den-building in the post war era:

I think most of the kids in those days loved building dens and lighting fires and stuff like that and we'd build dens all over the Forest, light our fires and sometimes we'd even go birds' nesting and try to cook the birds' eggs, if we got some eggs. We would eat things then just for the devilment of it, but which we wouldn't dream of doing now.

Thankfully, Peter Read is now a respected member of the Friends of Epping Forest, and actively promotes conservation of the Forest he loves! However, Peter was not alone, as another eminent member of the Friends of Epping Forest and the founder of the Suntrap Field Centre, Ken Hoy, also remembers an *al fresco* forest meal where he almost encountered the wrath of the then Superintendent, Colin Mackenzie:

I was ticked off by Mackenzie in the late 1930s for lighting a fire and cooking some bacon by the Wake Arms. He was terribly angry and I explained that I'd surrounded the fire with wet clay and we got a can of water ready to dowse down. Maybe it was the smell of the bacon that time but he mellowed in the end and said that when we'd finished our breakfast to put the fire out, and off he went!

Food of a very different kind was cooked by Jean Brazier who lived at Woodford, a wonderful example of the Forest inspiring a child's imagination in the 1940s:

Our playground was the Commons as we called it opposite our house, it had a pond in one corner which I think is called the Frying Pan and a big bush, a May bush nearby which we called May Ranch and that was the centre of most of our games. There were actually four bushes I think and it was very easy to make a bedroom and sitting room, I think we even had a veranda. I used to borrow my mother's brush and pan to go over and sweep the bushes out! We had marvellous games there.

The young Peter Read's imagination, of course, was set on far more exciting subjects inspired by visits to the Doric Cinema in Chingford which was situated on the corner of Station Road and Beresford Road. They would:

...see all kinds of films, like 'Sabu, the Elephant Boy', in the '50s this was. You'd have Tarzan and all these kinds of films- Tarzan and Sabu. They would set you alight, the Saturday morning matinees. We'd have a walk up there for the matinee, watch this stuff and then we'd be imagining it and reliving it all the way home. We never came home by bus in those days, we'd be walking through the Forest, so we'd come out of the back of the picture house at the Doric and go up Connaught Avenue, into the Forest there, and for that trip on the way home we might have been Sabu on one occasion or Tarzan on another.

For other children, the Forest was a magical place and the trees could become charms against mishap. Barbara Morris went to Woodford Green Primary School and she recalls one such tree that folklore says acts as a lightning conductor:

At the back of the school there is another tree, that is really dead, but its been struck by lightning about three or four times, and it saves the school and it helps to protect the school. That's what we were told when we were there. If you stand back to look at the tree you can see one of the branches that looks like the head of a bull.

Barbara Morris at the foot of the Blasted Oak behind Woodford Green Primary School. Sadly, the tree blew down in 2004.

She also remembers legends the children made up about their part of the Forest:

We used to play fairy rings, because there was a lot of mushrooms growing round in the Dell and as we were young, we thought there were fairies at the bottom there.

Imaginations could also be ignited through a trip on one of the rowing boats that used to grace Connaught Water, Hollow Pond and Highams Park Lake or by sailing model boats on the water. Stan Gailer recalls pleasant days out with his model yacht on Hollow Pond in the 1930s:

There was a boating lake for children's boats and we used to take my boat up there and sail it on the lake there. There were boats for rowing on the actual

Highams Park Lake, 1970.

lake, but I didn't go on those, I used to go round the back and there was a nice little pond there, just for kids. Sometimes, we would walk up to the Rising Sun where there was a little boating lake which children could go on, take their little rowing boat type of things. Opposite the Rising Sun was a very good tea place, serving ice creams in the Forest. So, that was one of the spots you'd go to because it was just a pleasant day out and we could come back to Leyton quite happily on the tram.

Many people can remember happy family outings to the Forest, events they look back on with great fondness. Mary Ashbridge - Taylor says:

In the 1930s my two sisters and I were lucky enough to have both a car and a car-driving mother and we made frequent afternoon visits from our home in Wanstead to our favourite spots in the Forest.

The brown-coloured box shaped 12 horsepower car, exciting to think of twelve horses pulling us along, was a Morris Cowley with a thermometer gauge in place of the mascot on the bonnet to give notice of the water overheating. Firstly we had to call at Randall's Garage in Church Path for petrol. Mr Randall asked the required number of gallons, at 11d [1] per gallon, and this was pumped by hand into a glass cylinder on top of the petrol pump before being disgorged down the hose pipe into the car. He then asked if Madam would like the windscreen and all other windows wiped, and the radiator topped up and the tyres checked. Payment plus a tip was made directly from the car and off we went.

Mother, three daughters and the dog, set off via Woodford High Road along Epping New Road, turned off at Long Bottom to take the prettier route up to the green-painted tea hut (this was not regarded as a suitable place for refreshments as the china crockery was washed up in a bucket of brown water at the side of the hut) on to High Beach. High Beach was the most popular destination except at the weekends and Bank Holidays when there were too many people and a great deal of litter. It was a wonderful open space covered with rabbit holes and the larger sandy fox burrows which caused tremendous excitement for the young dog Mickey, although the animals stayed securely underground. The excitement for us was the seemingly resident Wall's Ice Cream man with his "Stop Me and Buy One" tricycle. A snow-fruit in a three cornered cardboard case was one penny, an ice cream brick was twopence, a tub fourpence and a packet of wafers a halfpenny. An ice cream was a special treat.

---

[1] Eleven pence according to the pre-decimal coinage of pounds, shillings and pence.

After a High Beach stop we usually continued on through the Forest to where there was a favourite climbing tree. It was possible to stop anywhere and everywhere there were no restrictions. We used to pull down the lower branches of some trees for the dog to hold onto with his teeth, and there was nothing he liked better than to sail up and down at a considerable height. If allowed he would do this all the afternoon.

In the spring we took our tiddler nets to collect frog spawn from the ponds. In summer we made daisy-chains, held buttercups under our chins to see if we liked butter and, of course, everybody picked bunches of wild flowers. Later in the year it was fun to tread on puff-balls and to stick burs and goose grass on the backs of the unsuspecting. No visit to the Forest was complete without a game of hide-and-seek.

One of our annual outings was to take my Grandmother to gather bracken, as it was turning to autumn shades, for her vases. My Grandmother lived in a large Victorian house and before the bracken could be used it had to be dried and pressed by placing it, for many weeks, under the mats which were strewn about on top of the 'drawing room' carpet. I don't remember any of us suffering ill-effects from what is now described as a most poisonous plant, and the bracken stayed in the vases till the next autumn.

With my Grandmother on board we always took the route past High Beach Church which she thought was so beautiful and peaceful that she would like to be buried in the churchyard. Grandmother was not expected to climb the trees, but did enjoy watching the dog demonstrate his skills, and we used to drive to the Wake Arms and then take the longer route, with the trees forming leafy arches above our heads and a good chance of seeing deer in the clearings, through to Theydon Bois and down the winding lane to the picturesque bridge at Abridge.

Harry Berry, later to become a Mayor of Chingford, recalls a walk with his father when he was a very small boy:

My earliest memory was when my father used to take me on this 'seven fields walk' from the West Essex Golf Club to the Owl Inn, and I can remember in those days we were breeched. Little boys wore a frock until they were out of their nappies and that, and they wore frocks and little patented shoes as well. I can remember my father taking me on that walk, he used to take me regularly on that walk, it was quite a favourite one, and as we walked along a stone got in my shoe and I can remember him taking me to where he sat me down by one of the stiles there and took off this patent shoe and took the stone out. I could take you to that place now, and I was two! Not a bad memory and I can still picture myself in that little frock with those patent shoes; that would have been 1913.

More vivid memories are recalled by Marna Snook:

We lived in Rensbury Road, Walthamstow, and every other Sunday my Dad would put me on his bicycle and ride up to the Forest around the Rising Sun pub. Opposite was a green wooden tea hut and Dad always bought me a delicious ice cream. From there, we would wonder along through the Forest looking for acorns, or other bits of nature. Dad would tell me about the different trees and ponds. I would collect leaves and moss to take into school for the Nature Table.

There was a pond next to the Rising Sun, and we would use a net to catch newts. I would put them in a jam jar and take them home for Mum, who would promptly throw them in the garden! Sometimes Dad and I would cross the road to the area by Hollow Ponds. Here we would watch the swans and ducks, sometimes taking bread to feed them. Other times Dad would hire a rowing boat for an hour or so and I would marvel at the glinting water which was always clear and shallow enough for me to retrieve leaves, mud and even money from the bottom. Once I brought up a £5 note. Loads of money, back in the 60s! I remember one particular Sunday when Dad and I stalked a red squirrel. Silently and slowly, we got closer and closer. I nearly had it, but it shot up a tree just as I was about to grab it. I think Mum was relieved when I told her the story.

The cows that grazed the area were another scary time for a small girl. They were always enormous to me, and there was no way of stopping them from lumbering across the road to find the sweet grass. Often we would come through a clearing to be met by several beasts tugging at the bushes. I would freeze but Dad gently guided me around them, giving them a wide berth. In season, we would pick gorse, covered in deep yellow flowers, or take home may

Highams Park Lake in the winter

blossom, which stank but I thought quite pretty. Once, at Easter time we were caught by the Forest Ranger picking palm. Dad knew it was wrong, but explained I wanted a little of it for Mum. We had a light telling off, but still, Mum got the palm.

Winter and summer, Dad and I never missed our times together 'up the Forest'. Dad taught me a lot about it, the creatures that lived there, the cycle of nature and its dangers. I grew up acutely aware of textures, smells and seasons, and now at 49 I often pass by, thinking back to those glorious carefree days of adventure. I shall remember the exact routes we took and look wistfully at the space where the tea hut used to be. Dad has gone now, but I have treasured memories of our time in what I always feel is my part of the Forest.

In the winter, the lakes and ponds would sometimes freeze over. Beryl King, who lived with her Forest Keeper grandfather Mr Humphries at Knighton Wood, remembers hearing her relatives talking of one very important visitor who enjoyed skating:

I believe Teddy Roosevelt used to come over. I mean I can't remember that, it's before I was born, but they used to put all fairy lights in the trees round the lake and they used to be able to skate on it! Yes, you could skate in those days. I learnt to skate up there and my grandfather was a fine skater. It used to freeze over even after it went into the Forest and I remember they had to put the danger warning signs up, as the Lake was very deep in parts.

Sylvia Mason who lived in Woodford remembers skating, amongst other family memories:

In the winters when we had lots of snow, my father would take me to Connaught Water and we'd go skating. Swimming at the Whipps Cross Lido and later at the Kingfisher, Oak Hill. Many years after the War, on Whit Mondays, my aunts, uncles and cousins always met at the Royal Forest Hotel for picnics. Us youngsters played French cricket and rounders or paddled in the Lake. Sometimes we went to the fair. It was nice to see the cattle grazing (and so nice to see them back again last year), and we used to see who was first to hear the cuckoo. Many of the street children played hide and seek or jumping over the tank traps on Mill Plain.

The Second World War (1939 – 45) brought hardship and misery for many, but for some children living through the war the Forest provided them with many opportunities for adventure. Bill Embling was an ambulance driver and he remembers one such event:

The bomb disposal squad were very busy during the Blitz on London and I assume elsewhere in the East End of London. They would render a bomb safe, extract it and then transport it to a dump. They had such a dump on Chingford Plain where quite a number of bombs of assorted shapes and sizes lay surrounded by a barbed wire fence, and a small army truck would arrive with another trophy and depart. An area to keep away from, not for dear children who were as bad then as now. One early evening after school hours several children were seen running away from the bomb dump followed by a very loud bang. We heard later via the grape-vine that the little darlings had lit a fire in an open-ended bomb, and the sump being fairly close to the Forest, the blast blew every leaf off about 30 trees and the smell of all that chlorophyll is still with me today!

Not all children were such hell-raisers! As a youngster, Ken Hoy found a certain quiet freedom in the Forest that he could not find elsewhere:

I was what they call a late developer, I don't know if I was slightly dyslexic but I didn't learn to read until I was eleven whereas my sister was bright. So I had a bit of a thing about the fact that I couldn't read, and I compensated by drawing and going out in the Forest. I remember we had a stool with two finger holes in the top and by lying that on its side and covering myself with a carpet I could lie out in the garden with the carpet covering me and the robins and the starlings and the sparrows would come down and I used to watch them through the two holes, and that's the earliest memory I have. I can also remember sitting in the middle of a holly bush deep in the Forest and seeing a wren and a robin - it went on from there, I suppose.

I think it was the fact that I could get away from everybody else, and I was on my own, I think. I wasn't frightened of the Forest, or being alone. Although, I remember at one point, I must have been about twelve and I went out on my bike and I thought I would ride through the dark Forest, just to prove to myself that I wasn't scared of the dark, which of course proved that I was. Otherwise I wouldn't have done it! I think it was being alone that attracted me. I didn't have a lot of friends in those days. I was 15 before I had many bird watching friends who I used to go out with.

As an adult, Ken Hoy set up the acclaimed Suntrap Field Centre at High Beach which introduced thousands of Waltham Forest children to the wonders of nature, many of whom can still vividly remember Ken's enthusiasm and depth of knowledge. Beryl King's childhood was also closely connected to Epping Forest:

As a child I had to go and live on the Knighton Estate because I had quite a lot of illness and I needed the fresh air. My grandfather, Mr Humphries worked for Edward North Buxton and my parents, my mother at least, was born on the estate and they lived in Knightswood Cottage [2] which was at the bottom of Knighton Lane where it joins Monkhams Lane. That was when I was six years old until I was 13. Then I went back to my parents who lived in the Broadway

---

[2] Now demolished

Knightswood Cottage, Beryl King's childhood home

in Woodford. Then we were bombed out in 1941 and my father was badly injured and we had nowhere else to go, so we went into the cottage.

The cottage had two bedrooms, a scullery, a biggish kitchen and a living room, with an outside toilet, of course. The toilet had a water supply I can remember, but when they first moved in they had a water supply in the house but not in the toilet. The porch was covered with the Alexandra rose and we had blackcurrant bushes and raspberry bushes all round the house. We used to use my granny's old lace curtains to keep the birds off! For the toilet you used to have to come out of the door, go right round the back and it didn't happen to me, but one night my mother went round there and she sat in the lap of an old tramp. He used to go in there for warmth, into the water closet you see!

There were five paths from that cottage alone, up to the big house. At Christmas we not only had the red holly but we also had the variegated yellow, we used to pick it and take it indoors. Of course the people who worked on the estate were allowed to take a branch off the fir trees for a Christmas tree. Christmas was so un-commercial in those days, you know. I can remember we had to go to bed early and the Christmas tree wasn't dressed till Christmas Eve, now children are so blasé over Christmas. I used to attend Christmas parties at Knighton, at the big house, as a grandchild of one of the estate workers. These were run by the Buxtons for the estate worker's children. My granny used to go and help and I can see her now although it's a long while ago, in her white starched apron and on the top a little white mob cap. They used to rope them in to help with the children.

I'm not sure whether it was the Forest authorities or the Buxtons, but they used to give the estate workers the old fashioned clay pipe with a mouthpiece, I should think it was a good ten inches from the bowl of the pipe. A really long one, and that was a Christmas present, every year. We used it for blowing bubbles! There were none of those things that you got out of a tin in those days, you know. You used to have to beg for some soapy water.

I used to have my birthday party every year in the Forest; it was at the end of May I used to have the whole class from the Convent and there was a huge felled tree about half a mile from the cottage and we used to have parties up there. It was a marvellous time. I remember my mother's canteen of silver, when they were packing up one night (it all came from America because my father's mother was an American) and we all got home to the cottage and mother said to father "Where's the silver?" It was hanging on a branch in the Forest! If it had been there now it would have been gone, but he went back and it still hung there. I can remember going through Knighton Wood as a child to school, down to the Convent, I used to walk down there and back twice a day, right across the Forest which, of course, you couldn't do now.

We used to go fishing in the ponds, there was a lot of bamboo on the estate and my grandfather used to break off a bamboo shoot, tie a string on it and we used to go and fish for tiddlers! We did catch things, I believe there were quite good fish in that lake. I don't know if the fishermen still go there, but they used to go there regularly. I can remember a tree that was struck by lightning and it stood just like a Y, and all the children used to climb in the middle of it. And we used to have a big medlar tree on the estate, and we used to go there and pick the medlars, they were lovely, and blackberries and mushrooming and that sort of thing. There was a lot of arable land as well as the Forest part on the estate. Where the big lake is, where those houses are now, that was all arable land and he kept a lot of horses and cows.

Chapter 2 - The Second World War

Epping Forest played its part in the Second World War (1939 – 1945). It hosted army bases, Prisoner of War camps, barrage balloons and anti-aircraft guns. German soldiers parachuted to safety between the trees, and bombed out Eastenders were given shelter, first in make-shift accommodation and then, perhaps, in purpose-built pre-fabricated buildings. The memories of the people who lived through those years are sometimes sobering, sometimes heart-warming, but they all add up to a vivid picture of a country at war. September 7th 1940 was the first day of the Blitz and Ivy Alexander was in Epping Forest with her friend Rene:

I left school in the end of August 1940, we had been used to going to Epping Forest, quite frequently Rene and I. We would go every Saturday, whenever we could, whenever we could escape home. We'd cycle into Epping Forest and we hadn't been to Epping Forest the last week of August because there was a threat, or there was a rumour going around that the Germans were going to bomb Epping Forest and set it alight, as we had bombed areas in the Black Forest and set that alight. So we were too afraid to go to Epping Forest that week because we were afraid it might be bombed. But, we plucked up the courage. I was quite pleased to meet up with my school friend Rene, as not seeing her at school it was nice to meet. So we said, let's cycle into Epping Forest. I don't really know what time it was, it was about two o'clock I think, in the afternoon. It was September 7th.

The air raid siren went and we're in Epping Forest, and we've been in Epping Forest for a couple of hours and enjoying ourselves, and then the sirens went, but nothing happened in Epping Forest, it was quite OK. Then we saw lots of planes going over and we didn't know if they were English or German, or what planes they were, but there were loads, hundreds of planes. It seemed to be a continuous fleet of planes going over the Forest, going towards Stratford, going the direction of where we lived and then we saw planes being shot down and parachutists coming out of the planes and there were these air battles going on overhead. We dashed off on our bicycles, saying "we've got to rescue these poor people".

Well we were sixteen at the time, but of course we weren't allowed to, there were police and air raid wardens and soldiers and "Where are you going?" they said. "There are parachutists coming down" we said, but of course they knew, as they'd seen them.

There was shrapnel falling and we had to get under the trees to protect ourselves from shrapnel, it was pretty frightening. And then, when we came to go home, we saw what looked like big black clouds and we thought we were in for a storm, so innocent we were, We didn't think of air raids to the extent that had taken place, so we said "Oh dear, let's get home before the storm."

We really had difficulty in getting home. We couldn't get to Rene's house because there were air raid wardens saying there was a time bomb in front of her house. So we went to Gainsborough Road School which was behind where Renee lived and we had to be there for the a couple of hours. I wasn't allowed to leave it because of various time bombs and so on. In the end, I convinced the Warden to let me go home and Rene's brother helped me, he came with me. Eventually we reached home and when I got home my mother told me off like mad! "What do mean stopping out as late as this?" She told Eric, Rene's brother off, "You should be ashamed of yourself, keeping my daughter out!" He left my mother as quickly as he could and went home.

The next day I went to see Rene to see what had happened but she wasn't there because while they were in the Gainsborough Road School the time bomb blew up and blew her house up. So, I remember Epping Forest and the first day of the Blitz. That was September 7th, 1940 when I was in Epping Forest - those two things the first day of the Blitz and Epping Forest are imprinted on my mind. We'd had so many happy times in Epping Forest, but that day was really terrible.

Those people bombed out by the Blitz had to find refuge somewhere and Epping Forest provided a brief respite for some of the newly homeless. Gordon Forster remembers a walk in the Forest in 1940 when he:

…witnessed the bombed-out families from the East End seeking refuge in the Forest. Their encampment was amongst the trees on the left hand side of the

road going up to High Beach and some degree of privacy had been provided by the erection of a 6ft high Hessian "fence". This suggested some official organisation rather than a squatter's camp. No doubt it was only a temporary measure to deal with an acute crisis.

Joyce Casey was one of those evacuated to Epping Forest after the horrendous first night of the Blitz, she tells her story:

September the 7th in fact is when the air raids really started, and we'd gone round to my aunt's who lived in Canning Town. We went to the local market at Rathbone Street and came back and then the sirens went. People around us weren't used to the sirens going and we went outside into the garden, or the yard, as we didn't have gardens then, and we had the Anderson shelter there. People were bemused, what do we do? Then you could hear the drone of the aircraft and you looked up and you could actually see the bombs leaving the aeroplanes. Then there was the smoke and the noise and the fires, they were setting light to the docks which were only a few streets away. We went into the shelter and then, not thinking of the danger, we got out and I can remember seeing a parachutist coming down from one of the aircraft, and people were cheering because they thought it was one of the Germans and I remember my aunt saying "Stop cheering"- she didn't allow us to cheer because she said "That's some poor mother's son, that's coming down there."

Anyway that went on for quite a long time, the noise and the smoke, it was like a thick fog and my mother, my sister and I said, "Well we'd better go home." As we were walking back, we saw the people all coming from the docks and they were just walking, and they had this look of real shock on their faces, and they were pushing prams with goods in them. We walked very quickly and as soon as we got indoors my mother said, "We're going to pack something in our suitcases". She had these old cardboard suitcases. Then, the sirens went and we went down to the shelter. With everything being alight, the bombers knew their way, just follow the Thames, and it started again. And we sat there in the shelter and then we heard this terrific "sssshhh" and the bomb went off and my father said, "That's near."

The front of our house was all gone. It seemed so peculiar to see your bedroom with the wallpaper and the beds there for everybody to look at. We went to a local school, Holborn Road School, round the corner and we were told we had to stay there, and we were told at 6 o'clock that we were going to be evacuated and we went to Denmark Road School to wait for the red buses to come along, and we were told just get on the bus. "Where are we going?": "We can't tell you".

Joyce had a dog, Peggy, who she was desperate to take with her, the conductor refused until he realised that the young girl was so upset that she would refuse to go without her pet:

… the conductor said go on, take the dog, and I said she'll be very good! Anyway we continued and we didn't know where we were going, it was dusk by then and all of a sudden we had grass on either side and there were plains and trees and we were taken to what we later found out was the Butler's Retreat. We got off the buses, there were some women there, and we were then given two blankets each, a blanket to lie on and a blanket to cover over us, the men and boys went into one huge hut and the women and the girls were in the other. Anybody who had a dog had to tie it to the fence outside. Our dog was a collie, a very nervous dog, but we went out afterwards because I said to my mother, we can't leave her there, and we smuggled her back in and laid the blanket on the floor and covered the other one over us.

Then there was a terrific noise and evidently an incendiary bomb had been dropped just by the Queen Elizabeth's Hunting Lodge, which is now a pond. Anyway, the next morning they set up like a field kitchen and then there were women from Chingford who'd come along and they were issuing out clothes. Well, you have to remember that the majority of people just had the clothes that they stood up in and, you see, you didn't know where you were.

Joyce's family settled in Chingford, a completely different world from the working class Canning Town she had left behind. They eventually got a house at Drysdale Avenue and she remembers the contrast between her old home and the new one:

My father and mother rented a semi-detached house and it had a bath, we were used to having a tin bath in front of the fire. Now, we had a very large garden, and of course there were bungalows at the turnings at the side and they had

Butler's Retreat, Chingford

large gardens. So in front of us there was just open space, and at the back of that was the Forest so we had nothing to interrupt our view of the Forest and in the front was a turning, and looking out of the bedroom window was the reservoir, so it was a very open aspect, coming from a tiny terraced house. We occupied the lower part of the house because nobody was rich enough to have a whole house and we didn't have a garden we had a yard!

The end of the war resulted in a huge programme of house building for the returning soldiers and their families. Temporary accommodation was often required and the "pre-fabs" were a solution which offered housing built to much more luxurious standard than their new inhabitants had ever dreamed about! Elizabeth Hughes lived in one of the prefabs that were specially erected on Forest land at Wanstead Flats:

I moved to London [from Scotland] as soon as the war was over. When our husbands came out of the forces they only had a suit and £70. It took us two years to find housing. During that time we stayed with my husband's father and his new wife. These were tough times – we lived in one room with a gas mantle light, which was terrible, and we had mice so I kept all our food inside a tea chest. The toilet was outdoors and my family were very upset that I left Scotland as we had indoor toilets and electricity in the family home in Scotland. Our only hope of improving our living conditions was to get a council house but this was very difficult as you needed a certain number of points; and even with three families living in one house as we were, it still took two years to qualify. On my last visit to the council, the man told me I had no hope of a house; I was devastated and cried my eyes out. To our surprise, the following week we received a letter to inform us we had been allocated a prefab on Wanstead Flats. We moved in on November 4th 1946 and our rent was 18 shillings a week.

There were 200 of us living in prefabs on Wanstead Flats. I lived in one near the "sand hills" as they called them, although a lot of the sand was used for sand bags. My address was 56 Allanbrooke Gardens. All the streets, or "banjos ³" as we called them, were named after World War Two military generals.

We had everything we needed in the prefabs, and the council continued to add bits on to them while we lived there. Everything was electric which was good, except it meant things took ages to get going. It also meant we were badly affected by the power cuts; we were given one bag of coal a week which just drove up the chimney in no time.

During the "freeze-up" of winter 1947 our prefabs were terribly cold and used to ice up inside. We slept with all our clothes piled up on the beds to try and keep warm. At that time there was road building going on the German prisoners of war were helping with this – and there were piles of fence poles stacked up to use as fencing around the prefabs; my neighbour and I were desperate with the cold and crept out at night and stole some of the poles to use as fire wood. Our fireplaces were very small so the wood had to be chopped into very small pieces which we just couldn't manage to do, so we hid the poles in the wardrobe and under the beds. Eventually the electricity engineers came to try and sort the electrics out and they felt so sorry for us they helped us to chop the wood up so we could burn them and warm the prefabs up a bit. Despite the difficulties I think we were all very happy in our prefabs. My husband painted baskets of

---

³ Known as "banjos" as the streets were in a circular shape.

flowers in our living room and bedrooms and I built a rockery in the garden and polished the pipes until they gleamed.

The pre-fabs remained on the Flats until 1960 and Mrs Hughes remembers the camaraderie of living on the "banjos":

The wonderful thing about those days was the safety and trust; you could leave your keys under the mat without a worry. When we left and moved into our new place I realised I had left the girls' dressings gowns hanging up behind the bathroom door. I went back for them and there they were, still hanging there.

My husband organised the Coronation celebrations in 1953. Prince Philip once visited the area to open some playing fields – I still have a photograph of him walking along by our prefabs. We always celebrated New Year in the traditional Scottish way and had Beetle Drives. We loved our prefabs and kept them like palaces. There were also cows on the Flats every year and sometimes Gypsies with their horses. It was like living in the countryside and my daughters loved it. There was a pond right in front of our place and my youngest spent her days playing there.

Walter Barber was demobbed from the Catering Corps in 1945. For a while he and his wife and two small children lived with his father-in-law, but was delighted when his young family were allocated a prefab:

The prefab was in the American style and it was even complete with a refrigerator, which the English prefabs did not have. I had a reasonable amount of back garden and in it I kept chickens and rabbits, and there was sufficient play area for my children to allow me to put up a swing for them, and also plenty of room for me to grow vegetables and flowers. My wife was only too pleased to get any sort of accommodation, and when she first walked into the kitchen from the back door she just stood there open mouthed at the layout of it. Everything was put in, so that there was nothing you had to supply.

The heating was very good, there was a very small fire. I suppose no more than about 18 inches across, but that fire supplied hot water, (there was also an electric immersion heater you could switch on in the summer), and the fire

Some of the residents of the Wanstead Flats prefabs

burnt anything, potato peelings anything like that, it all used to go on the fire and get burned. There was an air duct from that fire to the two bedrooms and also an airing cupboard behind the fire where the hot water boiler was. It was amazing what they got in there, you know.

They took part of Wanstead Flats to build the prefab estate, it's opposite the Golden Fleece public house and the public house is between Whitta Road and The Chase, both roads are still there. All the prefab estate went up quite a decent way and there must have been nearly 350 prefabs there, they were all detached. All the prefabs were on their own concrete base so they were all individually placed.

Surprisingly, there was very little if any discordance amongst the neighbours:

In about 1957 somebody in Parliament said that that ground had been taken over under the Defence of the Realm Act and therefore, seeing as the Defence of the Realm Act was now finished, it should be returned to the Wanstead Flats and they should be cleared off. Two of us, myself and another house further over in Cunningham Gardens I think were the last two to go, and that was in

December 1960. The reason why I was holding out was that we had children of both sexes and we needed another bedroom and insisted on getting a three bedroom place.

The prefabs were taken down, dismantled properly and presumably there were assembled somewhere else, out in the country areas, because they could be decently resurrected. There's no trace of them over there at all; it's all returned to open grassland.

Wanstead Flats and Wanstead Park were both used for military purposes. Peter Reeve was a child during the war, living close to the Flats. He remembers the Prisoner of War Camp:

It spread from the boating lake over by Dames Road to Centre Road and Centre Road was blocked off to normal traffic and that was the entrance to it. All traffic had to go round Dames Road, Lakehouse Road to get to Wanstead. Most of the prisoners were in huts, there were some tents over there and, when there was a raid on, the prisoners were all out cheering the bombers on, you know! Some of the prisoners were marched to do jobs. What they did I don't really know, but you could see them under escort being marched along Capel Road, to various places where a bomb had dropped and they cleared debris and things like that.

It was behind barbed wire with high fences and we used to go and make faces at the prisoners and they retaliated by cheering the bombers on when there was a raid! It was all in good fun really, you know there was no sort of hostilities. We didn't treat them as hostile, they were prisoners in another country.

Beryl King, growing up in Knighton Wood says:

I can remember my mother daring me to go to Wanstead to near the prisoner of war camp. It was quite an attraction for these young girls. That was at Wanstead Park. I think they were mainly Italians, I don't really know as I was never allowed to go anywhere near them! Our own men of our own age were all away and I know two girls who actually married prisoners of war, after all they're human beings the same as us.

Allied troops were also stationed on Wanstead Flats. Peter Reeve remembers:

Towards the end of the war, just before D-Day a lot of Americans were stationed there in tented accommodation , just before the D-Day landings, and they used to get the gum out ("Have you got any gum, chum?") and they used to roam around. Apparently they were good lads in the pub, they would always buy drinks and that because the Americans were flush for money and that was another aspect that the Flats were used for. They were more the Aldersbrook Road end, there was another entrance at the Aldersbrook Road end into the encampment so the Americans went in that end and the prisoners went in at the Forest Gate end.

Chingford Plain housed Prisoners of War as well as troops, Peter Fitch recalls:

Chingford Plain saw some activity early in the war. Troops were billeted on the Plain; I can remember them very distinctly in Kipling-esque looking bell tents. In 1940 my brother and I could wander through the camp, there was no perimeter fence whatsoever, but eventually we were politely shooed off by an officer who came out of his tent. In due course some anti-aircraft battery appeared there with 3.7 inch guns and in 1941 or '42 more up to date anti-aircraft guns appeared. These were bigger guns which were more distinctive to me because they matched a gun on a battleship. It was in an enclosed turret, but I don't think the guns were ever fired in anger because this was pretty well after the Blitz.

Later, the camp housed some Italian prisoners of war. I'm never very clear whether it was in the meantime that Nissan huts appeared and a perimeter fence which was never very substantial. It may have been the Italians that first converted one of the mess huts there into a church, a small tower was put on it, but it was certainly there when the Germans took over later [4]. Of course the Italians must still have been there after we ceased fire with them, so they were hanging about there, but no doubt they were taken out to farms and things. Certainly a number of greenhouses in the Lea Valley had them working down there. I believe, but am not certain, that a very few of them did end up

[4] Barbara Ray in "Chingford Past" says that the chapel was erected by German soldiers and shows a photograph of it.
[5] Possibly after the Thomson machine gun used to shoot down gangs of hoodlums in prohibition America.

remaining and formed a nucleus of a relatively high profile Italian greenhouse owners in Lea Valley. They were a benign presence; nuns sometimes popped out of the convent which was on the edge of the Plain bearing gifts!
The Germans took over later but I cannot remember at any stage when there was any serious security there. I certainly remember walking past two prisoners working quite unsupervised by the Royal Oak pub near the bottom of Kings Head Hill.

Anti-aircraft guns were installed on Wanstead Flats and Bill Embling remembers that even these could produce some funny moments:

During the war there were anti V1 and V2 machines located on Wanstead Flats. We called these 'Chicago pianos'[5] and they were a series of rocket launchers which went off in rapid succession. During the day they were hidden in the bushes, and were brought out at night to be operated.

There were not that many working class women drivers in the fire service at that time but there was one stationed at Woodford, who was a greengrocer's daughter. One night, during blackout she was driving across the flats on a journey from Stratford and Woodford. Of course it was blackout so she couldn't see much. All of a sudden they fired one of these Chicago Pianos, as she was driving past! When she arrived back at Woodford Station, her language was such that I couldn't tell it to you, and she tore off her tin hat and said "Just as I was coming across the flats they fired a Chicago Piano, and it frightened the life out of me. Now, if you'll excuse me I must just go upstairs and change my knickers!"

Alan Hughes remembers more anti-aircraft equipment in the south of the Forest:

There were barrage balloons dotted around on the Flats and in school playgrounds and various other open sites. The main idea of the barrage balloon was it held the wire up which stopped low flying aircraft with precision bombing and also to stop them straffing which was a hobby of the German pilots. If they had run out of bombs they used to come in low and machine gun every thing in sight. The barrage balloon prevented that by having wires up that would ensnare the airplanes.

Also criss-crossed over the Flats were ditches, about 3 foot deep to stop planes landing on there, and the soil from the ditches was in big swiss rolls along the edge of the ditches so it sort of created a ditch and an obstacle above ground as well. I think most open sites like that had these ditches built across them to prevent aircraft landing. The swiss roll bits of earth were a joy for us youngsters to jump from one to another! It was good fun to see if you could make it from one to the next one. It was good until one day we landed on one which had a big wasps' nest on it! That sort of stopped us; we were more wary after that!

The Forest was also riddled with anti-tank defences; an attempt to stop possible German invaders reaching the countryside to the north of London. Mr Hughes recalls some on Mill Plain:

In 1940 we had just had Dunkirk, and England was in a desperate position. The Canadians made a big tank trap through the Forest, they dug it like a V-shaped dug-out so, when they were done, you'd never know. They blasted a lot of trees out of the Forest, which they had to do, to make it through. Its all been covered now, so you'd never know, but you can see where the path is - the path is still going down from Mill Plain down to the North Circular. You can still see the part that they filled in after the war. That was a big dip, or ditch, but on Mill Plain they had these tank traps, square built concrete things with the idea of stopping tanks, whether they would have done, one would never know, but a lot of things were done like that, in desperation I think rather than anything else, but we didn't know in 1940 how bad we were.

The young Alan Hughes, like so many other children during the war found adventure in their much-changed surroundings:

Another use that the Flats went to was that sand was excavated from the ponds and this went to be used for sandbags. The Sand Hills ponds had big mountains of sand around them, they were a real lot higher than they are nowadays. Just down from Wrigley Road there was a big pit dug and that was used to fill sand bags and they were distributed six to a road just in case you had a fire or an incendiary device dropped on you, you put a sandbag over it. I've just remembered some more things about the Sand Hills ponds. There was on the Aldersbrook Road side, some sand that was imported, I think, from Southend-on-Sea. We used to go over there with our parents to take a picnic,

Forest Keeper standing next to a bomb crater on Mill Plain.

take our buckets and spades and make sandcastles because it was fine sand, sea side sand, and on the steep side on the south side of the Sand Hill ponds we used to watch despatch riders training. They used to ride up and down over the steep side and over the top and they used to spend hours doing that in their preliminary training, and that was good entertainment for us kids in those days.

There was a bandstand up on the corner of Capel Road and Centre Road and all the wood from bombed out houses was put in there and people could go and take it for fuel or repairs to bombed houses and children used to delight in bringing a few bits of wood home to put on the fire to eke the coal ration out!

Alexander Longmoor and his friends found other uses for the debris that he remembers being in the Bandstand Pond:

That was filled up with all sorts of debris from the Blitz, timber and wire and rope and all bits and pieces and it was a great afternoon out for us boys to try to make a raft to actually paddle across the pond.

Hilda Anslow spent most of her war years as a Land Girl, working at Woodredon Farm, then Carrolls Farm and Birds Farm in the High Beach and Sewardstone areas:

One job on the farm was cutting kale for the cows. This grew about 5ft. tall and had very large leaves where rain or dew was collected. I had to cut this from about 6 inches above the ground and even on a sunny day my left arm was soaked, so I collected up the hessian sacks and bound them round my arm with binder twine for a bit of protection. The cut kale was collected and carefully loaded on to a horse and cart and then we set the horse in the right direction and left her to get on with it, while we gradually pulled the kale out, a stick at a time, and spread it across the field, with the cows following us munching happily away; they loved it. They weren't tidy eaters though, they would start eating one piece, and then wander off to another leaving a trail of destruction behind them.

Many people lost their lives during the War, but for others life was only just beginning. Some of these babies started their lives in ambulances on the roads of the Forest as Bill Embling remembers:

During the war most of the maternity hospitals/casualty hospitals in the Epping Forest Area were turned into air-raid shelters. So, pregnant mums had to go by ambulance to St Margaret's in Epping and of course, the black-out meant no headlamps in cars, so it could take ages to get to Epping. Time after time, babies were delivered in the ambulance before arriving at Epping, and the language of the ambulance drivers when they returned with the soiled laundry was not to be listened to!

The echoes of World War Two could still be heard even in the last few years of the twentieth century as unexploded bombs were found and detonated to make them safe. Alf Wright worked for Epping Forest from 1965 to 1991 and can remember one such incident:

One night a World War Two German plane was shot down and crashed in the Forest alongside Lodge Road, (more commonly know as the "hip-dips" as the road goes up and down in two humps) just off the Epping New Road. I was 13 years old and the following morning, in the company of my friends, we went to the crash site where we found firemen damping down the hole in the ground and making safe the Forest growth around it.

Many years later I became an employee of the Corporation of London working as a woodman/tractor driver in Epping Forest. My duties at that time included the collection of litter in the north end of the Forest. The site in which the plane crashed was then being used as a landfill for the litter, which was being collected.

Some years after that the Corporation of London was contacted by a club which was interested in digging up the aircraft engines in the site, and they were in due course granted permission to do so. However, they found not only both engines but also a bomb fin. They immediately informed the Forest Keepers at The Warren and the bomb disposal squad from the Territorial Army were called in to deal with the matter. There were two bombs which hung on the wings of the plane.

I was now a Forest Keeper and I was on duty at the site the day they found the bombs. They used a JCB for digging which took them about a week. On the day the bombs were found there was a loud crash with the driver shouting that he had found them. The Epping New Road was immediately closed off. The TA steamed out the high explosive in the bombs effectively and both bombs were removed from the site.

Chapter 3 - Clubs and Organisations

Epping Forest has provided a fascinating resource for both formal and informal education. Brian Brenchley grew up in Forest Gate in the 1940s and '50s:

I joined the Boy Scouts and at various times we would trek to a campsite at Debden Green. The campsite was on the very edge of Epping Forest, and here we would practise the many skills that we had learnt. On arrival at the camp we would be split into small groups. One to set up the tents and site, another to prepare the fire site for the cooking and a third to go and collect the wood for the fire. No gas burners in those days; everything was cooked on an open wood fire. The procedure for collecting the wood was for four scouts to go into the Forest, find two long straight pieces of wood then lash them together stretcher style. Two scouts would carry them along whilst the other two would pick up wood and place it on the "stretcher". When full it was carried back to the campsite and the fire lit. This was a chore that had to be done every day, if not then we would not have any cooked food. As we had to go further afield each day, before setting off we had to take a compass bearing in order to find our way back. Some years later after I had left the Boy Scouts and joined the Air Training Corps, we used to use Epping Forest for our map-reading and escape and evasion exercise.

In 1919 the Boy Scouts Association set up headquarters at Gilwell Park on the edge of the Forest and many generations of scouts and guides have camped there and have been introduced to the Forest. For local boys such as Peter Read, Gilwell offered many adventures. He can remember the lure of the swimming pool:

It was very useful in the summer of course, and if you are dressed to go swimming no one knows whether you're a scout or not – or a cub! And our gang would creep up there, get through the fence take our clothes off with just our cossie, just our costume on and we'd creep over to the swimming pool and splash about with the other kids. Sometimes, all the scouts and cubs in those days used to have an obligatory knife or staff on them, and often on our way home we found we had one of their knives or one of their staves on us! So, we had quite a good time up there, there was always something going on at Gilwell Park and it was such a big place, and youngsters make friends easily and we made temporary friends with lots of the scouts.

One day we went up to Gillwell Park, creeping around the out-buildings there like we did as kids, and we came across this whacking great big saddle. It was a really ornate saddle, with a big silver pommel and braided stirrups hanging down, I can't remember if it was carving or burn-carving that was on the saddle; it took two of us to lift it and we lugged it through the Forest. I'm talking about when I was 7 or 8 years old; I can't remember exactly. But we took this saddle down and put it on a horse. We were galloping around on the horse, all day and all night. We left the thing there and we'd come in at night, when our mums and dads were busy. We always came in black as the ace of spades, always mud all over us and especially me, covered in cow pats or horse mess! On this particular occasion we didn't have the cinch tied up tight, and I remember hanging on to the saddle as the whole thing slipped round and I'm hanging on the underneath of this horse! We eventually left it with the horse galloping off; it galloped off with our saddle hanging off beneath him.

You can imagine our surprise about a week or so later when our mums were reading the Chingford Guardian saying that Baden Powell's saddle was found, the saddle which he used in the relief of Mafeking which he'd brought over and which was on show up there was stolen and later found tied round a Shetland Pony at the bottom of the road!

The Woodcraft Folk was set up in 1925 to help working class children access the countryside for their health and well-being. There were local clubs in Leyton, Leytonstone, Walthamstow, East Ham and Hackney; and Epping Forest was their bit of the country. Irene Poole has been involved with the Woodcraft Folk all her life:

I first became acquainted with Epping Forest really when my father started a Woodcraft group in East Ham in 1934. And within a few weeks of starting, we started camping at High Beach and we camped with another group because we had no equipment. Sunday mornings we used to go swimming in a forest pool on the Wakes Arms road. I suppose about 10 or 15 youngsters would go, some of whom had never seen the countryside, because in East Ham people were very parochial and often didn't move out of their immediate area. During the war we camped at Pipers Farm and then, during this time our Sunday hikes during the winter would take us up through the Forest. We used to go to Loughton on the number 20 bus and we'd walk up from Loughton, usually stop at Ernie's for a cup of tea or coffee or whatever and then carry on through the Forest. Ernie's was at a junction up from the Robin Hood, going up to High Beach.

In about 1946/7 East Ham Borough Council bought a farm at Debden:

As I understand it, Councillor Jack Hart, who was the chair of Education at the time, had seen the advertisement of the farm for sale, realised it was on the edge of the Forest and at the time the borough were wanting to build some new secondary schools and he wondered if the City of London would exchange the Debden farm for the triangle at Manor Park. The triangle made by Forest View Road, and the Rabbits Road, would have suited a school campus, but they wouldn't agree to the exchange. So, from then on the farm was developed, we helped to pull down the cow sheds and so on and Debden House became the camp site and the house became an education centre, and we've camped there ever since and of course it's on the edge of the Forest, and so the Forest is a major part of the activities.

Tania Collins has also been involved in the Woodcraft Folk all her life:

As none of us had cars in those days, we all travelled by bus or train to Debden and then carried what we needed up to our field at the top which was surrounded on two sides by the Forest. Field Five was one of only two fields where you could light fires, and each area had their own permanent square, cut for the fires. East Ham and Leyton were at the top of the field with the Forest behind us and Waltham Forest, Harlow and Mitcham were on the other Forest side. We were all alongside the Forest and we all had our own exits through the barbed wire, which became a bit enlarged for easy access into the Forest. Also there was a ditch around the field and because we all used it so much this became a way for other people to use as well, because we used the reeds and that. The only negative aspect about camping next to the Forest was the gnat bites, because of the ditch and the large boggy areas, as soon as it became twilight we had to quickly put on our long trousers and long-sleeved jumpers or else you were bitten all over. After the Whitsun camp which lasted three days, instead of the usual weekend, we used to sit in school counting our gnat bites, my record was 107!

Once a year on the Sunday of the Whitsun weekend we had permission to turf a camp fire in the middle of the field for a large camp fire for all the Woodcraft groups and many other campers from the other fields joined in as well, it was an annual event. Large pieces of wood would be bought from the Rangers and a group of macho men would spend all day chopping the wood to the right size, chopping notches at either end to balance the wood and to build a large pyramid fire and in the old days Woodcrafters did a fire dance around the fires. Woodcrafters are based on the American Indians' "traditions". The worst part about cooking on wood fires was scrubbing the black soot off the cooking pans at the end of each weekend, they had to be done before they were put away.

One of our favourite walks was due north of our camp site where we reached the tank traps. This was a long large ditch dug during the war which was now covered with plants and great for climbing in and out of. Then we would spend long afternoons playing games in the Forest, run outs could be played anywhere on hikes, or at camp as all you needed was a certain tree as your base to return to. The favourite game at Debden which would last all afternoon was called "pirates over the border". There was a large rectangular area where bracken grew freely and lots of trees and a path through the middle. Two teams would have either side as their area, choose a secret den and put three sticks in the ground in the den, and then each team would sneak over their border to try to find the den and take a stick. Anyone captured became a prisoner and was put in the den and they could also be rescued and so the game could go on for ever and ever, or until all three sticks were captured. I returned recently and the whole area was completely overgrown, nobody plays there anymore.

The Friends of Epping Forest was founded in 1968. It is a group concerned with the conservation of the Forest that lobbies the Conservators on management issues as well as providing a host of social occasions, walks and talks. Ken Hoy [6] remembers that one of

[6] Founder of the Suntrap Field Centre

the reasons why it was set up was to articulate concerns over horse riding:

When I began teaching at the Retreat [7] in the '60s the damage in the Bury Wood was terrible. Trying to walk children through it in the winter made me very angry and I wrote a letter to the paper about it. There was quite a controversy going on at the time. Alfred Qvist [8] obviously read those letters and invited me and one or two others to a meeting with horse riders and John Biggs-Davidson [9] up at the Wake Arms and the Verderers and Qvist asked if I would take them, being familiar with the Forest and out in it every day, if I would take them to the muddy areas. So we went through the muddy parts of the Forest to see the horse riding damage where it was bad. Then at the end of that tour in the car park Sir William Addison, who was just William Addison then, said it was important that the Conservators weren't seen as an anti-horse riding group; that we needed the other Forest-users to give their opinions so that the Conservators could act as the impartial chairman and see what was to be done about it.

That was the basis on which we set up the Friends of Epping Forest, and in 1968 it was a sort of federated organisation, 15 organisations affiliated themselves to the newly-formed Friends and all the secretaries and chairmen met occasionally. The Eastern Sports Council invited us to the Council Offices in Loughton, to talk about the damage that the horse riding caused and from then the Eastern Sports Council recommended that a licensing scheme be introduced and as you know still, what 30, 35 odd years later it's still just about to come into operation!

So, it was the horse riding damage - but, of course later we were also very concerned about the M25 coming in down through Theydon and we became very involved in what was called the "Alliance against the M16", that's what the M25 was called in those days. We again formed a big alliance of local organisations and we've been involved with public enquiries ever since then, roads are the major threat to the Forest in my view now.

I think we give a sort of friendly support, I think. We have this role where, if

[7] Jubilee Retreat, Chingford (see Chapter 4).
[8] Superintendent of Epping Forest
[9] M.P. for Epping Forest

the need ever arises, for example over traffic and road problems, we can give evidence to a Public Inquiry. There was a time back in the '60s and '70s when the Forest Committee tended to adopt the view that something outside the Forest couldn't be considered by them or they couldn't take action on it because it was outside their remit. Well, of course that's broadened now, they are concerned with the whole area and environment around the Forest and that's good. But, in the early days we had to console ourselves with giving evidence to Public Inquiries and influencing public opinion in ways that perhaps the Corporation wasn't able to do - as they saw it in those days. That has changed a little bit now but I still think we have an important role to fulfil, in fact our constitution does allow us to "organise and influence public opinion" and that is one of the major roles that we have, in support of the Epping Forest Act.

Harry Bitten is a very active member of the Friends of Epping Forest. He tells of the lobbying that is part of the Friends' purpose:

I joined the Friends of Epping Forest but in an inactive way and I think probably my membership lapsed for several years. But I got seriously involved when the Conservators, suddenly without any public consultation, proposed to develop a golf course on the eastern half of Chingford Plain, this was in 1980. As I said, there had been no public consultation and we only got to hear about it through a mention in the local rag. I think the only consultation was with the members of the Chingford Golf Club because a lot of the people in that Club and the Royal Epping Forest Club were very much in favour of a course for the public, as distinct from the other public course on the western half of Chingford Plain.

The Conservators had acquired a grant from the Eastern Sports Council and had started cutting fairways onto the Plain before we had started to get our act together and oppose it. We organised a petition by carting a petition around on Chingford Plain at the week-ends and in no time at all got, I think it was 9,000 signatures, which we presented to the Conservators.

We also organised a walk on Chingford Plain to protest against the proposed golf course. We weren't allowed to hold a demonstration, it was against the byelaws, it was said. I think we thought that there were a thousand odd people at this protest walk, although, the Keepers downgraded it somewhat to about three hundred. I'm sure it was more than that. We weren't allowed to put up a banner, so we rushed into Station Road, Chingford and bought some terry towelling which we daubed with marker pens into a series of letters and we put those on our backs and stood in a line and the resultant message was, "No Golf Course Here." We had to be very careful about how we arranged these things in case we said something rude which would probably be against the byelaws.

There was a public meeting in Spicer Hall in Chingford which was packed with people mostly protesting about the idea of having another golf course on Chingford Plain, but with a few golfers present who were obviously in favour of the idea. Verderer Bob Mitchell was on the platform and he was the only one that came out publicly against the idea of a golf course. The other Verderers took the view that since the Epping Forest and Open Spaces Committee as a whole had voted for it, they were bound to adhere to the views of the majority, even though they probably privately didn't think it was a good idea. Anyway, Bob Mitchell stood up to be counted. All this aggro led to a certain amount of mild vandalism on the present golf course. I had a visit from a golfer policeman who tried to lecture me on these bad actions but, "It wasn't me guv" I said, and I can only think that people who were sufficiently incensed with the idea that a golf course on another part of Chingford Plain was an imposition that they took it a bit further than most of us would have taken it."

At the Epping Forest and Open Spaces Committee, after there had been all kinds of protests against it conveyed to the Conservators, Bob Mitchell was on his way back from Canada on that same morning, but Georgina Green who was the Secretary of Friends at that time, was urged to contact him to attend the meeting before going home, which he did and voted against it and the thing was voted down after some "argy bargy." I think probably some members of the Epping Forest & Open Spaces Committee didn't like us very much as a result of this, but I think that we healed the rift by the following year organising the Epping Forest Victoria Centenary Celebrations in 1982.

Chapter 4 - Celebrations

1978 saw the centenary of the Epping Forest Act which charged the Corporation of London with the care of the Forest. Keith Howes was Senior Conservation Officer in the British Museum's medal department. He enjoyed making medals and decided that he would create a centenary medal, not for commercial purposes, but in appreciation of the Forest:

I hit on the idea of putting Queen Elizabeth's Hunting Lodge on the obverse alongside the head of a deer and, for the reverse, I decided that the bark of the beech tree would be appropriate. The next thing was – who would fund it? The first person I approached for funding was Sir William Addison, Verderer of Epping Forest, then Deputy Lieutenant of Essex and author of 19 books on Essex. He appeared off-hand and asked irrelevant questions and I believe he thought I was a nut case, and I could hear that he was recording the call!

Unfortunately, funding was not forthcoming from any other sources either so Keith and a friend, Peter Shorer, decided to proceed alone. Profits from the medals they sold were used to fund the production of others and he gave free copies to various local institutions and people including the Duke of Gloucester, the British Museum, the Goldsmiths Company, Redbridge Library, the Guildhall, Queen Elizabeth's Hunting Lodge and John Betjeman:

Then, out of the blue I got a letter from the Remembrancer [10] 'requesting the pleasure of the company of Mr and Mrs K. A. Howes' at a garden party at The Warren, Loughton, on Tues 23rd May 1978. So I was to present a medal to the Duke of Gloucester. However I was requested not to inscribe the edge of the medal with "presented to" but leave it blank, as were the rest. Came the day and I ordered a taxi for my wife and we duly arrived in style at The Warren to be put in a grand marquee on the lawn with, of all people, Sir William Addison. We eyed one another but not a word was spoken. Minutes later the Duke of Gloucester arrived and walked to a pillared microphone and to my

---

[10] The Rembrancer is in charge of the Corporation's hospitality and ceremonial occasions.

amazement the Remembrancer called me first, and as I walked towards the Duke I had a short speech ready in my pocket. However, it wasn't necessary as the Duke knew me well as he was often in my workshop, being a trustee of the Museum and the Coin Department in particular. We just carried on talking and when I returned to my wife I said my short speech wasn't necessary, to which she replied "No, but we heard every word you said as the microphone had been left open". After this we partook of fairy cakes and tea served on gold plated cups with a military band playing in the background. Unfortunately, our taxi didn't return and we were eventually driven home in a police car which didn't please my wife, so we were dropped in the next street to avoid the neighbours!

That week the local Guardian newspaper printed the design of my medal at the top of every page and I was delighted by that. I didn't want to make any money out of it, I just wanted to join in the festivities as Epping Forest has meant a hell of a lot to me.

In 1977 Fred Matthews of the *West Essex Ramblers* and Harry Bitten of *the Friends of Epping Forest* were approached by Newham Council to devise a walk through the Forest to celebrate the centenary of the Epping Forest Act. The *Centenary Walk* is still published today and every September a very large group of ramblers joins Harry to walk the route:

As a consequence of writing the walk, Fred Matthews and I and our respective wives were invited to the Garden Party to celebrate the Centenary of the Forest. This was at The Warren. We were then standing about with a glass in one hand and a large creamy cake in the other and in due course the Ranger, The Duke of Gloucester, who was on the other side of the lawn, came over towards everybody and Fred, dear old Fred, decided that the Duke was heading straight for him and he thought it would be very difficult for him to do anything with all these cream cakes in his hand and he put his hand behind him, backed away and bumped into the Lady Mayoress of Walthamstow! The cake was plastered all over the back of his coat, but the Lady Mayoress was up to this task and got a kind of device for removing cake from the back of someone's jacket out of her handbag and started scraping this stuff off for him. But, the Duke veered off at the last minute and went down to the end of the line and gradually started working his way up the line, being introduced to people by Mr Qvist, the Superintendent.

Unfortunately when the Duke arrived opposite Fred and I, Qvist hadn't the foggiest idea who we were and asked the Duke to wait a minute and rushed off to find somebody who could say who these two strange people were! Well, the Duke looked at us and we looked at the Duke and thought "Well, there's not much point in us gawping at each other" and we started chatting and said that we were only there because of the fact that we had produced this book about the Centenary Walk in the Forest, and the Duke started chatting back to us. Qvist returned, looking very askance at us for having spoken to Royalty without being properly introduced; and at this time the Duke was asking "Do you have any problem in the Forest with these cattle wandering, do the cattle ever attack walkers?" Whereupon Qvist said, "No Sir, they're not entire [11]," to which the Duke replied, "What?", much to Mr Qvist's embarrassment. Eventually the penny dropped!

In 1982 the Epping Forest area celebrated the 100th anniversary of Queen Victoria's visit to Epping Forest when she declared the Forest to be protected for the people's use. The biggest and most possibly the best remembered, is the Friends of Epping Forest's Victorian Fair on Chingford Plain. Harry Bitten and his wife Peggy were on the organising committee:

We went so far as to hire a coach and horses so that we could convey Vera Bonner in the guise of Queen Victoria from Chingford Station on to Chingford Plain. We decided that we wouldn't stick to the actual day which was a Thursday the 6th May, we decided to hold the celebration on the 8th May because it was a weekend, a Saturday and we decided to hold it on Chingford Plain because of all the logistic problems holding it where the original ceremony took place in High Beach. On the great day there was a massive activity in Chingford with Vera Bonner in her coach, accompanied by John Bonner, her husband, going well beyond the call of duty by wearing a kilt and pretending to be John Brown. They set off from Chingford and met a huge parade that had been organised to start from Chingford Green, consisting of The Chingford Pipe Band and various groups like that. There were girls voted

---

[11] They had been castrated

"Miss Waltham Forest" and "Miss Chingford" and "Miss Woodford" and "Miss" something else, all delightful young ladies waving their wands and things and that progressed onto Chingford Plain, and in due course Sir William Addison, who was President of Friends at that time, made a welcoming speech and then the day progressed with lots of people dressed up in Victorian costumes. We had archery, a football match, tug of war, a mass jog, a cycle run; all kind of activities, as well as hundreds of stalls selling things, and roasted a series of lambs. It was a wonderful day and remembered by everybody who went. We re-enacted the Battle of the Alma - a group came forward called The Thin Red Line who offered to re-enact the battle of the Alma. So, anyway, that was a great day.

'Queen Victoria' heads the procession from Chingford Station to Chingford Plain during the Centenary Celebrations of 1982.

Chapter 5 - Recreation

Over the last 125 years the Forest has been used by many thousands of people for organised sporting activities. Golf is played at Chingford, cricket is played on Forest land at Woodford Green and the football pitches at Wanstead Flats are always popular in winter. Runners are often seen around Chingford Plain, usually members of the Orion Harriers Club. Ron Bond, a member of the Club describes his sport:

On most Saturday and Sunday afternoons from September to March the Forest is threaded by several hundred runners. Some by themselves or in small groups keenly intent on training; some running easily and sociably together, while others are racing, sometimes in large numbers strung out over a considerable distance in an inter-club or league match. As a 17 year old cross country runner, living in Ilford, my first encounters with the sport in Epping Forest were in 1953 in Woodford Green Athletic Club's schools race from the Woodford Green Men's Club on the corner of Links Road on the High Road, and in the County of London Senior Scouts' Championships at Gilwell Park, Waltham Holy Cross.

Football on Wanstead Flats, c1970

Alexander Longmoor remembers a use for the Forest ponds now forbidden by the byelaws:

On a very hot afternoon if we weren't at school one of the pleasures that people used to do was to come over to the Leg Of Mutton Pond in Wanstead Park and go swimming in it. It was a swimming pond, it was provided for swimming and it had a diving board, a changing room and toilets, you can still see the foundations there. But it wasn't one of my favourite things as I didn't like the mud and the sharp stones that you had to walk on. They reckoned that one young person dived off the board and got stuck in the mud and basically by the time they got him or her out they were dead. From that point on they took the diving boards down and knocked down the changing rooms and all the rest of it and put up notices saying "No Swimming", which are still there today in any of the ponds in Wanstead Park.

Alan Sibley remembers people swimming in Forest ponds:

The Wake Valley Pond, now that had a diving board on it, my uncle used to live in Chingford was a keen cyclist and he used to go up there on his bike, and swim. He would dive from the diving board into the pond, how often he did it I don't know. It must have been deep enough to swim in, the Wake Valley Pond. A number of these ponds were bomb craters that got filled with water, but that diving board was purposely built for people to use, and that's something I remember as a kid.

Alan is now the Forest's Voluntary Fishing Bailiff, he has fished in the Forest all his life and has been involved in local angling clubs. His is a familiar and well liked face in the Forest, he tells how he became the bailiff:

Somewhere around about 1995 my angling club was approached with a view to looking after one of the local ponds, the Wake Valley. They were having a considerable amount of problems there with litter and vandalism and that sort of thing, and they thought it might be a good idea if a club took over the running of it and put Bailiffs on the water and everything like that. So we met up and we did eventually take a licence on the Wake Valley Pond and, with a little bit of hard work and effort from a number of club members, we did manage to bring the litter problem under control and the vandalism and make one or two efforts to clear the place up and made it environmentally better.

At present Alan is the only Voluntary Fishing Bailiff for the Forest. One of his tasks is to educate new generations through training days:

We've done a couple [of days] at Wanstead Park and we've done a couple at Connaught Water. Connaught Water wasn't a major success this year with the weather conditions as they were, it was so hot, being a shallow lake and that the fish were not very keen on biting, but the children they did have a lot of fun.

Jane White attended a very unusual party in the late 1980s:

We had great fun when we were invited to a party on the ice on Connaught Waters, on the ice in the middle of the pond. The friends who organised the party were Dick and Christine Williams. They phoned and they said; "They used to have ice fairs on the Thames so we're going to have a picnic on Connaught Water." We got there and they really did have an enormous blazing fire going and I must say it was with great trepidation that I went onto the ice at Connaught Water. In the end, hoping it wasn't going to break; but there were so many people on already that I didn't think it would. But the bonfire was an extraordinary thing as it had melted itself a small puddle of water perhaps an ice or two inches deep, but it was still blazing merrily and we had mulled wine and sausages cooked on sticks round this fire, and there were potatoes baking at the edge of the water, at the edge of this little pond. Dick has 12 grandchildren and there were the grandchildren, all skating and tobogganing all skating over the water in the light of this enormous fire and it really was the jolliest evening! All the children will remember it for the rest of their lives, as I haven't ever had a picnic on a pond in the middle of the water on the ice and it was their jolly idea that made it such fun.

For some children, however, their experiences of sport in the Forest was not always positive. Richard Fitch was a pupil at Hackney Downs Grammar School in the late 1950s:

We were often taken to Epping Forest for our cross-country runs around

Bonfire on Connaught Water, part of the barbeque attended by Jane White (pictured centre).

Chingford Plain. The changing rooms were located in "Jubilee Retreat", known to every schoolboy as the "Jubilee Cowshed", as the cows could have been removed just before we arrived! I remember a large, crumbling wooden building with rows of benches, and an area for after race ablutions. This consisted of old, free-standing cast iron baths containing always scalding hot water, which in reality, especially if you came last, was tepid, dirty brown liquid, with a substantial layer of mud in the bottom. Ah, happy days!

Cyclists have also been part of the Forest's history, from the annual Epping to Woodford fancy dress procession in Edwardian times to the mountain bikers of today. Stan Gailer remembers his experience of cycling in the Forest:

I got a bike when I was about 15 years old, it was my uncle's bike, he was one of the ones who came back from Dunkirk and he gave me his bike. I was then evacuated to Brentwood, during the war. But, I had a bike, so I used to come home on the bike from Brentwood which was very nice. Then I used to ride up and down those hills at Hollow Ponds, they were lovely to go round the Hollow Ponds on the bike, a wonderful experience!

In the days when bicycles were luxury items, Peter Read and his gang of friends from the Yardley Hill Estate found alternative forms of transport:

In those days you were very lucky to have a bike, no one ever bought you a bike from a bike shop, you got a couple of wheels somewhere, and if you could only find a couple of pram wheels you made yourself a trolley, what we'd call a trolley. This was two sets of pram wheels, a plank of wood in between them and the spindle was pulled by two pieces of rope which was how you steered the thing.

We'd use our trolleys or our track bikes and come over the Switchbacks and down Pole Hill; we'd called it Pole Hill, really its Daisy Plain. Daisy Plain is after the slopes of Pole Hill. A block of wood acted as your brakes, although usually it was my shoes, and I usually got a good hiding when I got home!

We went tobogganing as well, that's a beautiful tobogganing place and, you'll never believe this, but the Friends of Epping Forest printed a Christmas card two years ago with people tobogganing down there with their grandchildren. And that granddad was my pal, one of the same boys I was tobogganing with then at the age of six or seven! So, there's this Christmas card from the Friends of Epping Forest showing these two blokes and their grandchildren and he used to go down there himself – that's great!

A sport of a different kind, and illegal in Epping Forest, was practised by Peter Read until the 1980's. Now totally reformed, he remembers his time as a poacher:

I was creeping about and getting into shooting a bit more, or poaching if you like, and I was over Roddick's Field. I used to have all of Roddick's to myself, as Roddick couldn't see you from his house, he lived the other side of the hill. I used to walk up to the top of the hill, look down on Roddick's House, (this is Andy Roddick the old farmer) at 5 o'clock in the morning and he'd be wheeling the old milk churns out ready for the lorry of the Milk Marketing Board to take his milk away. If ever he'd see me on the sky line, he never came after me, although sometimes he'd give you a shout if he was near you, and you'd get off. I had a lot of respect for Roddick and I've got a lot of respect for Michael

Davies [12]. They were the only two farmers that I was aware of who owned a bit of land round here.

I'd have pigeons, rabbits, pheasants, partridges all taken with my silencer or my snare and I'd go as far as Green Lane, over Trueloves, that was a beautiful place to go, Trueloves. Even now the grass grows about that high. You walk over Trueloves and that place is stiff with pheasants, stiff with them. As you walk through the Green Lanes themselves with all the hawthorn bushes that's were those pheasants sit, they sit along the green rides. They're in that field during the day and they go in the ditch when it's a bit frosty, or if they think the fox is going to have them they get up in the hawthorns.

Not all physical exercise is of a sporting kind! One wonders how many children have been conceived in the Forest over the past hundred years! Eric Marwood has a funny story from the 1950's:

In those days you could go where you liked in the Forest, I think these days there are logs across every entrance. You could drive in there and do your bit of courting. I remember my brother- in- law had to call the AA out because he was up there with my sister and he sort of got stuck in the mud in there, bit embarrassing I suppose!

The Speedway Track at High Beach was a phenomenon for twenty years in the mid-twentieth century. Today the track, behind the King's Oak Hotel at High Beach, is grassed over and the Information Centre and Field Studies Centre stand where once the bikes roared.

Roy Delaney is a speedway enthusiast who loves to share his knowledge of an historic site:

It all began on the 19th February 1928, when the first official speedway meeting in England was held there behind the Kings Oak Hotel on the old disused athletic track. It was generally known as the King's Oak Speedway.

The promoter Jack Hill Bailey of the Ilford Motor Company was gambling on a crowd of 3,000, but all roads leading to High Beach were jammed packed by

---

[12] Michael Davies is a Verderer for the Forest and is quoted in the "Agriculture" chapter.

Alan Stewart at High Beach

9.30 a.m. thanks to an estimated crowd of 30,000. All entrance tickets and programmes had been sold, and the barriers leading to the track had been pushed over, the barbed wire fence surrounding the ground was also cut down to allow the non paying surging people into the arena. The high beech trees which stood back from the track area were soon filled with the enthusiastic fans. An historic day indeed for two-wheeled sport.

Racing continued at the Loughton track well into the late 1940s, until the manager of the Kings Oak Hotel decided to close the track as the dust from the meetings was fouling the swimming pool. Following this decision, hundreds of fans signed petitions which were handed to the owner of the hotel, but to no avail. An elderly fan said to me at the 2004 reunion, "Forget the pub – speedway was the real Kings Oak."

Alan Stewart was a rider at the speedway. He loved his hobby, until he met a woman in the crowd who he discovered he loved more. He describes the thrill of the race:

On arrival the paddock marshal came over and gave Ted, my pusher off, his copy of the programme so we could see what heats we were in. That led to a quick appraisal of our chances of success as everybody knew their mates and the chaps who you rode against so you could tell if you could beat them, as well as them knowing that they could beat you!

Later on, the paddock marshal came round again and handed you a bag in which there were a blue and a red and a white and a yellow ball, and you put your hand in the bag and drew one out and whatever colour you'd drawn that was the helmet colour and gave you your position 1-4 on the track. So if you had the inside position, which was red, you were better off than someone who had drawn the number 4 against the fence on the outside of the track.

At that stage, the paddock master gave you your riding colours, the waistcoat you rode in to be identified by the spectators. Suddenly, well to put it bluntly, the stomach distended! You got a sense of fear; it was like going down in a lift. You didn't show it, obviously, but you felt it and that persisted until the preceding race to the one you were going to ride and, when it was over, the paddock gates were open and the old riders came into the pits and you went out. Ted Gower and Ken Cobbin would push my bike and I'd walk out, we'd walk up to the starting gate and, believe you me, at that stage apprehension was on you like nobody's business. After the announcement was made through the loud speaker to the crowd "The next race is..." the riders names, and blah blah blah, I'd get on the bike. Ted would switch on the fuel I'd tickle the carburettor and we'd bump start and I'd fire the engine.

Well, all four riders did a complete [practice] lap and believe me again while you were doing that lap, coming round to the starting gate again the feeling of apprehension came again– what was going to happen, were you going to have an accident, would you get killed or break a leg? When you came up to the starting tapes, you'd touch the front wheel against the tapes. Once the race had started then the feeling of apprehension went. You hadn't got time for wondering about what was going to happen, you just had to try to make sure that you did your best, and that was it. After the finish you returned to the pits, take off your jacket, wash your mouth out, do what you could to disgorge cinders going down your neck. It was very dusty, as the track was made of cinders.

If you did come unstuck, then your face was a bit vulnerable, so I did wear a chin-guard but that's about the lot. If you were unlucky and you were drawn out to ride where you got two rides consecutively, then that was just too bad. Believe you me, when you'd done four laps at High Beach, which I never liked particularly because it was a circular track, and it was more or less on the go all the way, you were tired out. A conventional track has two straights and two bends and you got a brief respite, but I remember at High Beach when we came back into the pits if anyone had given me a glassful of water or lemonade or whatever, my hand was shaking and I'd slop most of it away.

You can't hear anything at all when the race is on, you can hear as you shove off and cruise back to the pits, you can hear the crowd applauding. There was always people hanging over the pits wanting your autograph, but the point I should make is that even if there were no crowd, the average rider would still ride. You're not really interested in the crowd, it's part of the spectacle, but just riding against each other is enough.

Speedway became a national craze, with even the big film stars of the day cashing in on its ability to pull in audiences at cinemas. Alan Hughes came across the shooting of a film at the Speedway when he was a young boy:

It was the 1940s, during the school holidays. I was out with my friends having a ride out and we saw all these policemen walking about and we asked what it was all about, and they said "They're making a sequence for a George Formby film, go across and have a look at the cycle track". So we went over and we saw them, and they

Stuntmen at High Beach Speedway

were only doing it about a week or ten days. We spoke to George Formby, who was well known years ago in the film world, and we saw him do a lot of these scenes, and they did a lot more than they actually used, it was quite interesting to see a lot of extras, or doubles rather, but we did see the guy himself.

It took about a week to film a five minute sequence. The actors came every day from Ealing, coach loads of extras or people dressed as policemen for the film and they were there for over a week. I think we went up about three or four times, my friends and I and we saw them doing it. They built things [ramps etc] in the ground, and they burnt them down [as part of the film stunts] and rebuilt them, so it took a long time to film the scene on the sequence.

Jack Farmer worked as a mechanic at Theydon Bois. He remembers visiting the first speedway meeting and the fascination the bikes held for a young man just starting out in the world of motors:

There was one old boy, he was a bit of a joker, I think he rode alright, though, but once the race was over he'd come round on a tiny little bike. Frank Brennan and I would watch from the trees. It was something new, something different that's why it attracted such big crowds. We used to spend all our dinner times polishing the parts and the engines just to get an extra half mile out of them. You'd polish the fly wheels, but you mustn't overdo it otherwise you might have thrown it out of balance.

Chapter 6 – The Outdoor Classroom

Many local people experienced a school trip to Epping Forest where they were introduced to the wonders of nature at one of the education centres that have been set up in the last fifty years. Fred Speakman's pioneering centres at the Jubilee Retreat, Chingford, then at Roserville Retreat in High Beach, have now gone but the Suntrap Field Centre run by the London Borough of Waltham Forest, the Epping Forest Centenary Trust and the Epping Forest Field Centre run on behalf of the Corporation of London by the Field Studies Council still welcome thousands of children every year.

Ken Hoy MBE was a primary school teacher in Chingford who had always enjoyed his nature studies class. His interest in environmental studies, a term he helped to coin, led him to leave school-based education in 1962 when the perfect job became vacant for him:

I saw an advertisement in the press for a teacher to run a field centre in Chingford at Jubilee Retreat and I applied for that and to my amazement, thinking you know, there'd been lots of applications, I got it! There hadn't actually been another application; in fact the job had been advertised for months. It was the place where Fred Speakman had started and then he moved up to Roserville, at High Beach, and the Jubilee centre became vacant. When I began it was a dreadful snowy winter in 1963 and it became so bad that the toilets were frozen!

I was left alone there. Fortunately, once you were appointed to a post like that you were considered the expert and there was nobody to tell you what to do. So, you had a free hand, and during that period when you didn't have so many classes because of the weather I remember thinking, you know, what is this all about? We've got the Forest here and I'm supposed to use it, how can I best use it and what can the Forest offer? Of course I mustn't do anything that can be done back in school, its got to be something specific to education in the Forest, and it was from that basis that I began to think about it and eventually when I got a couple of inspectors coming along and seeing Fred Speakman and I they decided to separate us a bit, so that we had different schools. I had known of

Fred. He was a naturalist who happened to be a teacher and I think I was a teacher who happened to be a naturalist, and so I was very keen to have the teachers come to work with me - previously the class teachers had not accompanied the children. Two very good teachers did come about '64 or '65 and then Suntrap was put on offer to me in '67 and we began to get more help with other class teachers coming and a bigger field-teaching staff and it went on from there.

Suntrap was an old maternity hospital at High Beach:

Expansion was offered to Waltham Forest originally in 1966, the story is quite interesting. One day at Jubilee Retreat it was snowing and outside in the yard was a tall man standing there who I recognised as Alfred Qvist [13]. The snow was coming down, so I went out and asked him if he'd like to come in. He said he was waiting for Dr. Stevens, that's the Education Officer for Waltham Forest, who hadn't turned up - so I invited him in. He spent an hour and a half with some kids from Mission Grove, a Walthamstow High Street school who converted him. They didn't know who he was so they just chatted to him and I was getting quite embarrassed all the things they were telling him, all about fox tracks and all about the Forest's history and all sorts of other stuff and in the end he went away highly amused and full of chocolate biscuits and marmite sandwiches!

The Epping Forest Committee and the London Borough of Waltham Forest decided that Ken needed a purpose built centre at Jubilee Retreat in which to carry on his work. However this idea fell through when, a Miss Brenton of High Beach offered them Suntrap as a gift in 1967 and the educational establishment moved locations.

It was a wonderful job so much so that I always felt guilty that I'd got a job that sort of cheated. It wasn't a proper job; I was getting paid for it but I was out in the Forest all day! I still have that feeling that I've not done a good day's work in my life, because since I left teaching in Chingford I've gone into the Forest and it hasn't been work.

I had a free hand and I had to think up what sort of things we could do,

---

[13] Superintendent of Epping Forest from 1949 to 1978

anything from poetry and drama to pure natural history. I wanted to do things that were best done within a glade in the Forest, with all the atmosphere, not things that could be done back in the classroom. So we had a huge broad canvas and we worked from that and when there were more teachers at Suntrap - we went up in twos. First four, then six ,eight, ten and finally twelve teachers. I insisted that we put on offer to the class teacher 150% of what it was possible to do. They had to make a choice of what they wanted and that meant there was variety every day. The weather changed, the class changed, the place we went to changed, the time of year changed so it didn't become stereotyped or stale and we had a very varied and flexible flowing programme.

The Epping Forest Field Studies Centre [14] opened on the site of the old Speedway at High Beach in 1971; Paul Moxey was the first Warden:

I think it's worth saying something about the philosophy behind it, because if there's any one man's name (and I'm delighted to say that it is now actually commemorated on the building) it was Alfred Qvist. He was Superintendent at the time, a kind of larger than life figure. I was fortunate in that the centre was his idea and I was in charge of it. I was running something in the Forest but I was not a member of his staff and I got on with him extremely well, I had pretty free access to him and he had access to me. He was very friendly and gave me lots of advice but beyond that I was a relatively young man. Not my first job but probably the biggest job I'd held so far. He was within sight of retirement (he retired in '78) although he actually worked on through official retirement age to see through the official celebrations of the centenary of the Epping Forest Act.

1970 had been designated European Conservation Year and Alfred Qvist wanted the Centre to be the Corporation's contribution to the year. He wanted something tangible that would last and make a practical contribution. He wanted it to provide a teaching service for schools, he wanted young people to know about and appreciate the Forest. He wanted it to be an information point for visitors. Initially that was just an information desk but it extended into a programme of walks and lectures and so forth. There was a vague aspiration, but it turned into reality, that it would act as a centre for research, attracting

---

[14] Run by the Field Studies Council

and promoting research into the Forest and feeding that information back to the Conservators so they could use it in practical terms for management. He had the vision and the political skill to get it through committees, and get the financial backing for it. It was opened in June '71 by Prince William of Gloucester, the son of the Ranger, the Duke of Gloucester.

To start with, we had a very simple introduction to the Forest for primary schools. It was stressed to us that many of these kids came from an urban background, not many were local schools. It would be an exaggeration to say that they didn't know what a tree was, but they certainly didn't know what a beech was, as opposed to an oak or a silver birch. They didn't have the simple identification skills. We'd do simple things, like looking for insects in the grass during summer, or pond-dipping.

For senior classes what we did bore little resemblance to the syllabus- tied courses now. Some of them are so eclectic really when you look at it, it's extraordinary. We actually did have groups that came out to do industrial archaeology. An awful lot did urban studies comparing Harlow New Town with Waltham Abbey. A bit later on we took courses down to Docklands and London City Airport looking at changes in the geography of East London, and there was a lot of focus on Loughton Brook.

Chapter 7 – People...

There are many people who contributed significantly to the Forest in the 20th century. Some of these key characters are described elsewhere in this book, others are actually speaking, more are given their own space here.

Fred Speakman was a naturalist, teacher and author. He taught generations of children at his education centre at High Beach and among his books are 'A Keeper's Tale', 'A Poachers Tale' and 'The Forest by Night'. Before he started the nature study centre he taught Alan Hughes at his school in Upper Walthamstow:

I remember school outings as kids. We went in the 1930s by train to Chingford and walked up Fairmead Bottom, up to maybe the Owl, but certainly the Robin Hood, as an expedition. Our teacher Mr Fred Speakman, was well known. He used to live at High Beach, but he came from Walthamstow. He lived at High Beach latterly and he was a great naturalist. He used to take us on these trips with our wellingtons, and take us there, we never got lost mind, it was quite something to bring 50 or 60 children to the Forest. Still we did it and we had lunch, we'd take our food with us, but we had nothing else: that was our entertainment!

Speakman loved the Forest at any time of year and even in the middle of the night, as David Gannicot discovered:

When badgers were much more common in the Forest, I often went with my brother or a friend to a sett in Epping Forest to await their nocturnal explorations for food. Since badgers have a keen sense of danger, it is necessary to settle down quietly in the Forest about an hour before dark if you want to see them. To a young lad, the Forest could be quite eerie with the trees taking on weird shapes as total darkness approached.

The date was the late 1940s and the sett was about half a mile off Goldings Hill. One evening, having patiently sat still for a couple of hours, we heard a quiet padding noise from our rear. We assumed a badger had left a different sett to the one we were observing. The muffled sound continued for several minutes and I began to think it was not being made by a badger. Suddenly, out of the darkness a human figure appeared. He had made hardly a sound. The man was Fred Speakman, a local naturalist. We didn't see any badgers that particular evening but were thrilled to have met this knowledgeable man.

Peter Read got to know Speakman personally and can remember a very gentle and knowledgeable man:

I used to go up to Speakmans' quite a lot. If I'd been shooting and I had some pigeons and they were no good to me, they'd feed his badger and his fox. He had a tameish badger in a cage out the back which he called Treacle, and he had a fox, which I forget the name of now, but it was a lovely fox.

He was a very unassuming fellow, didn't put himself about, very, very quiet, and I got on well with him. He was a nature study teacher, he used to teach nature study from Roserville Retreat, but the Suntrap took over and Ken Hoy started to run the Suntrap, and gradually all the kids were going to the Suntrap rather than his place. He wanted his badger to go to Suntrap and I remember once going up and getting Treacle, the badger, in the back of my Land Rover in a big cage and took it down to Ken's and, as Ken took it out I remember him shouting "Watch your leg, he'll have your leg off!" and they could. They're ruddy powerful things and if this thing bit your leg you'd know all about it, it could take your foot off. I certainly got to know a lot about badgers from him, from Fred. He was a lovely man.

Paul Moxey, (first Warden of the Epping Forest Field Centre, remembers) Alfred Qvist whose idea the Field Studies Centre was:

Qvist was quite big in the world of land management and he was well into conservation, probably more than many of his contemporaries, and he believed in networking before anyone had invented the term. I didn't quite stand in dread of him, although I know many of his staff did. He did all his committee work and he did a lot of committee work in other parts of the country too. He used to ride his horse out in the early morning, drop in on the work force, see how things were going on before getting down to his paperwork or going into the Guildhall. He must always have been changing out of riding boots into city suits.

For John Harvey, former MP for Walthamstow East and Verderer of Epping Forest from 1970 to 1998 the following were key characters:

Looking back over the years, one of the persons that had a great impact on the Corporation in terms of the Forest was the man who was Chairman for many years; a fishmonger in the city of London who was a member of the worshipful Company of Fishmongers. Sam Sheppard was a delightful personality and he remained Chairman for a long time and he was very forthright in his views about the interest in the Forest. There is no doubt in my mind that at a very difficult time in the post war changes, he was able to ensure a high regard for the Epping Forest Committee on the part of various members of the Corporation itself.

Sir William Addison

There is of course the considerable contribution made by Verderer Sir William Addison who not only was interested in everything to do with the Forest, he was also a writer of distinction, and his books on the Forest are necessary reading to anyone who wants to delve into the past history and the continuity of history in the Forest.

I think the Forest has been fortunate in its selection of people who have taken a great personal interest in it. Bernard Ward for instance was a Verderer of great distinction, immensely knowledgeable about everything to do with the flora and fauna of the Forest. He really had been of great value and we were indeed fortunate in a way when he died, to find Michael Davies, a local farmer who was virtually able to take over much of the thinking and the hard work that Bernard Ward had done over the years. He was 20 years a Verderer.

Sheppard's Meadow next to Bell Common is named after Sam Sheppard who, as John Harvey mentioned, was Chairman of the Epping Forest Committee for 16 years. He interviewed John Besent for the post of Superintendent in 1978 and left a lasting memory on the interviewee:

Sam Shepherd

Sam Sheppard was synonymous with Epping Forest. He was a Billingsgate fish merchant and had a very broad Cockney accent. He wasn't like the traditional committee member. He was all powerful at the Forest. He'd been Committee Chairman for 16 years and I remember that he was on my interviewing panel. One of the questions I asked was would I be my own boss? I didn't want to report to anybody else other than the Town Clerk and that wasn't clear. He replied, in a broad Cockney accent, "You'll be yer own gaffer!" Nobody else would have said that..

Another bluff old gentleman was the late Duke William of Gloucester, the Ranger of Epping Forest. Verderer Eric Dormer remembers one interesting encounter he once heard of from a former Committee member:

The Ranger was not known for his conversational ability and I was told by my friend, that one of the things you dreaded was a function where the Duke was present. The Chairman would come up to you and say, "Please go and talk to the Duke for a bit", but the question was of course, what did you say? He thought, my friend, that he would perhaps carry on a conversation about the cattle and the fact that they wandered down into the streets adjacent to the Forest into people's gardens eating their flowers, but he didn't get too far because he barely started when the Duke looked up at him and just said [gruffly] – "Tell them to shut the bloody gates!" And that was the end of that.

At the other end of the social scale were the tramps who used to inhabit the Forest and who were often well known to local people. Beryl King can remember Peggy Wooden Leg whose death was even reported with sadness by local newspapers:

There used to be an old tramp called Peggy Wooden Leg, he used to come to the cottage for old clothes, he used to live in the Forest, he always lived in the Forest and he had a stump, and of course you can imagine the children and how they went on with him, but my father and my grandfather used to give him all their old clothes. He was a regular tramp. He used to live in the Forest towards the Napier Arms, that way, and he used to go down to the Convent for his breakfast in the morning. He was harmless, but of course sometimes he got stroppy with the children and he used to take his leg off! You know what children are.

Irene McIntosh also remembers Peg Leg:

I lived from the late '20s to mid '30s in Brookscroft Road in Walthamstow and I remember when the dustbins were put out for the refuse men, a man known as Peg Leg Pete obviously because of his wooden leg, had a rummage through the bins looking for things he could either use or sell. One thing I do remember was him taking a rather ugly and ornate vase from next door's bin. He was quite tall and wore a cap and had a beard. I understand from my father that he had a hut of sorts in the Forest; where I don't know.

Chapter 8 - ... and Places

For many people a visit to the Forest usually included a drink in one of the public houses. Some are still there, others have vanished and some like the Owl at High Beach have been rebuilt. Harry Berry can remember the "Old Owl" well before the Second World War and a joke that even today we are familiar with:

We could take our lunch, buy a drink, sit in the large hut or what I preferred, was to sit on a bench in the grounds and enjoy a lovely view. There was a large water butt under the hut with a large notice inviting us to see the "water otter". The first time I saw the notice I dashed over to see this wonderful creature only to find suspended in the water a "hot water bottle"!

The old Owl pub at High Beach, now demolished.

Stan Gailer has a special place in his heart for Turpin's Cave, a pub off Wellington Hill. Now a private house, it offered the chance to see the supposed hideout of Dick Turpin the infamous highwayman, although the Cave was most likely bogus. At 18 years old Mr Gailer

joined the Salvation Army and enjoyed cycling with some of the group:

We cycled to the Forest quite a bit, and then one day we found a little pub called Dick Turpin's Cave, it was near High Beach. You just go down a hundred yards from the pub there [The King's Oak] and then down a hill and there was this little pub down the bottom. It was a lovely pub, there was only one bar as I remember, they only sold beer and soft drinks, no spirits or wine, and it was so friendly. There used to be a crowd of cyclists go there, they used to go in and then somebody would start singing a song and they all joined in. We didn't drink much, I think we had about half a pint, 'cos we couldn't afford much, I was only 16 or 17, 17 or 18 and so it was a wonderful little pub. Of course other people could go there on the 35 bus, but it seemed to be mainly youngsters on bikes in the pub in those days.

After serving in the Second World War, Mr Gailer often returned to Turpin's Cave:

I came back in 1947 and started cycling again. We then cycled through and found the pub again, by then there weren't many cyclists, it was mainly motor cyclists, but again it was still a very good, very pleasant pub to be in, very happy. There was a lovely crowd again, and they even gave us jam sandwiches, they passed jam sandwiches around. Of course, coming back from the forces we knew more songs and we knew all the old songs and there was a youngish crowd and it was a really good sing-song there.

Peter Read also visited Turpin's Cave:

I used to have a look round Dick Turpin's Cave which is still there and the pub was there also and you could go up to the pub in them days and get a bottle of pop, or an arrowroot biscuit or something like that and have a look round the cave. There's not much there in the cave in the first place, it's just like a chalk dug-out if anything; but at least you had a packet of crisps as you're staring and looking at it.

On the corner of Church Road and Lippitt's Hill there lie "the Catacombs", a Victorian folly which were once open to the public as

The "Catacombs".

"roman ruins". Peter Read remembers visiting them as a boy, and the first time he set eyes on ...

... our Norman Castle , or what we called our Norman Castle in those days. It's actually a folly in the grounds of Lippitts Hill Lodge. I got in there in 1953 when I was 10 and my name is still carved there to this day. It's literally an old Victorian folly, people say it's made out of the stones of Chelmsford Jail. When you walk in, the whole thing goes right down into the earth with little air windows every now and then for air to draw down into the tunnels which spread out everywhere. I remember going down one tunnel and coming up the other side of the house.

We used to get in this place, no one ever came out and chased us off and I remember going down tunnels a long way, really a long way and I really am surprised thinking about it now. I remember being given the day off school at one time, probably for the Queen's Coronation, in 1953. Well, I was about 10 at the time, and that's the day we went there and carved our names all over the place and we really spent the whole day messing about down there in these tunnels and going all over the place, and that was great.

Peter's gang of friends also enjoyed visiting Queen Elizabeth's Hunting Lodge on Rangers Road. Until the 1980s it contained a museum of natural history and archaeology:

The thing that fascinated us kids was all the little bits in there. There was an old deer in there, I don't know if it's still there now but it was well worn and threadbare on the back where people used to sit on it! There were all little knick knacks behind glass display cabinets, I remember, and one of them used to be a Verderer's knife. We didn't realise what it was. It was a bone handled knife, but the end curled round a little bit. Nearly all the kids in our class or our gang or whatever, would all be saying that one day they were going to get the knife out of that case and be off with it!

Also what I liked, what fascinated me up there was the traps, the gin traps up there, but best of all there was a man trap up there. It was a bloody great big man trap about a yard wide with big teeth on it and I've always been fascinated with anything clockwork or " ingenious", which is where the gin trap got its name from.

One hundred years ago the "Retreats" of Epping Forest were very well known to inhabitants of London's East End. Now, they are almost forgotten. The Retreats were refreshment houses set up by local entrepreneurs who knew that the many organisations who visited the Forest each year, such as Mothers Unions, Sunday Schools, and works outings were reluctant to obtain refreshments at public houses, which many of them objected to on ethical grounds. Big wooden buildings sprang up around the Forest, at Theydon Bois, Loughton, Chingford, Buckhurst Hill and High Beach. They provided teas and often fun fair type amusements, donkey rides and a piano for sing-songs. Some Retreats were operating until World War Two and memories such as these from Constance Hoe bring the Retreats back to life for us:

My husband [15] and I were brought up in Limehouse. Every summer Mr Baldock from a church in Kerbey Street, Poplar, visited every Chinese house in our area that had children. He issued tickets to each child for a day out to Chingford.

---

[15] Leslie

We were told to be at Poplar railway station at a certain time; and made our way to Chingford by train.

Arriving at Chingford we all walked up the hill to the Jubilee Retreat. Here we were once again given tickets for free rides on the helter-skelter and roundabouts. We had to bring our own packed lunch but were given tea in a big hut. Watercress sandwiches, buns and so on. Tea was poured out from big brown pots. After spending all our free tickets we went into the Forest climbing trees and going for walks with our friends. Some mothers used to come bringing their babies. Although there were over 100 children I can never remember anyone getting left behind or lost. Opposite the Retreat on the edge of the Forest a gypsy was pulling up a reed like plant, folding back the long leaves on the stem of the plants and plaiting them to the ends of the leaves to form a whip, which he sold to us children for a few pence.

My husband who is now 85 can even remember how sad he felt when he got up too late to meet at Poplar Station. It did not occur to his mother to take him to Chingford herself. Once the Chingford day was over all the children used to look forward to the next year's outing, and the Chingford Day was talked about for weeks afterwards.

The Shaftesbury Retreat on Shaftesbury Road in Loughton was run by the Shaftesbury Society to provide days out for children from the East End. Ivy Alexander [16] was just one of many thousands of children who visited this Retreat:

I went to a school called Bidder Street Infants and Junior School and that was in old Canning Town. Once a year the whole school, well I don't suppose the Infants went, but the junior part went to Loughton. We'd go by train from Canning Town Station to Loughton Station and it was thought about with great excitement. The night before we all had a bath, a special bath, you all had to be clean and put on your best clothes. We'd get the old zinc bath from the yard, hanging up on the wall of the back yard, and we'd all have a bath and then we were given a little bit of pocket money and promised that if we didn't behave ourselves we wouldn't be able to go, so it was a great event, once a year, and it was a terrific outing for the whole school.

---

[16] Author of "Maid in West Ham"

The manager's house at Shaftesbury Retreat, the only part that remains.

Before we went we all had blue discs, I remember, a disc which we put round our necks and on it, it had something about the Ragged School Union. I've since discovered that it was the Shaftesbury Society that organised the Ragged School Union and so I suppose the Ragged School paid for these outings, but everybody had a disc around their neck and we used to laugh "Ragged School Union! What's that? What's it got to do with us?", But of course there was us with holes in our shoes and holes in our clothes – but "Ragged School Union? – no way!"

We would go in crocodile fashion from one end of the town to another and singing all the way, one song we used to sing was "It's a long way to Lousy Loughton, it's a long way to go" we called it 'Lousy Loughton' we didn't know why but it was alliterative and it sounded nice. We had a special train, parents didn't come with us of course, but they all waved us off at the station. Everybody would be hanging out of their windows, all along Stevenson Street, I can still see that, all waving. We were singing all the way of course, and sticking our heads out of the train window and getting told off!

Joyce Casey also went to the Shaftesbury Retreat with her school, its interesting to compare the two ladies' memories, so individual and yet so similar. Mrs Casey says:

My first recollections of Epping Forest was at the age of eight or nine when I went to a local school and we were told that we would be going to Loughton, and we were to go home and ask our parents if this was OK. We were going by train, staying there for the day and then returning by train. I went home very excited and told my parents, and they said yes that was quite all right and I could go. At that time I had already been on a train, but not many children where we lived had been on trains so there was a great buzz of excitement.

Prior to the day when we were going to Loughton we were given this disc, it was blue with a hole on the top, made of cardboard about the size of a car tax disk. You had to pin it to your dress or your jersey. On this blue disk were the words the Ragged Schools Union and it had your name. My mother wasn't very happy about this, my sister was even more scathing, and anyway the day arrived when we were going on the train.

My mother took me to the school that day because after all we were going on the train, and being away for a day. We were all very excited, jostling one another and talking very loudly and then we assembled and we walked down to the station and got on the train. The train in those days had compartments which had tight seats with the luggage rack above and it was netted. But if you climbed onto the seat you could look into the next compartment, so you can imagine all these excited children getting themselves onto the luggage rack hanging out of the windows, because after all we weren't all health and safety then, you just got on with it. There was yelling and punching and "I want to go here" and "I want to go there". Anyway we arrived at 'Lousy Loughton' because that is what we called it, we didn't know why it was called 'Lousy Loughton' we thought that the people there were lousy. I've subsequently found out that they thought we were lousy!

When we got off the train and we were told that we had to be very quiet and we had to walk along very quietly, and so we did. We were very subdued but we were all bubbling with excitement inside so we walked along until we came to a clearing in the Forest and we entered this gate, and there was a kiosk in the middle and then we went into this building and we sat down on the wooden benches with wooden tables in front. There we were given a sandwich, and it seemed to be that it was dried bread with corned beef or paste or something in it, and a glass of water, and we had to have it blessed.

Ivy Alexander remembers arriving at the retreat buildings:

They were like big sheds, and we were led in and sat on big forms and just given things to eat, pies and anything, and of course we ate what ever was put before us! And then, after that we were led into the Forest. I suppose they were some people there organising us, but I don't remember being organised in the Forest, I just remember running about and getting lost and everything was strange. You see, we were used to judging distances by friends' houses, but once we were in the Forest we didn't know where we were - one tree was the same as another tree!

And then we were collected at the end of the day and taken back for tea and roll call and it was then that we could buy certain things, they had shops and we could spend our pocket money to buy things for those back home. We'd buy silly things like hair slides and whistles, collar studs things like that. Then we went back on the train, singing all the way and all the family were waiting for us on the platform cheering and it was a lovely day, it really was. People always remembered going to Loughton, and the people at Loughton said that it was called 'Lousy Loughton' as all these scruffy dirty children came from the East End, and the place was littered and filthy, and they had to disinfect the streets after we'd all gone. But, we didn't think, that it got its name that way, for us it was just a word, we said 'Lousy Loughton' like people say 'Sunny Southend'. We sang 'Lousy Loughton.'

Joyce Casey continues her story:

After we'd eaten [lunch] they then said "We're taking you to the Forest". So we were taken to the Forest and there we were playing rounders and various other games. I remember going to a pond and seeing all these tadpoles and the frogspawn and everybody was getting very excited about it, of course we all wanted to take some of it - Canning Town would be alive with frogs! But of course there was no way to take any. We were going in the water and coming out and here again there was no one to tell us not to, we were just free spirits.

I presume that the teachers were around, but I have no memories of anybody saying you shouldn't do this or you shouldn't do that. Anyway, after a couple of hours or so we were rounded up and then we all walked back to where we were going to have tea.

You can imagine all these children who had been clean at the beginning of the day were now covered in mud splashes and socks were down, and ribbons had come out of your hair and so forth! We went back and had a current bun and a drink. We milled around the kiosk that sold sweets and then we all had to walk back very quietly and demurely down to the station and we all got back on the train. But the difference to the morning was that we were all very tired after being out in the open air and running around and everybody was quiet and some were falling asleep. Nobody worried about getting up onto the luggage rack, nobody worried about pulling the strap down and pulling the window down and hanging out of the windows. Then we came back to the station and went back to the school, and there my mother and sister were waiting for me and we went home and I was telling them about this day in the Forest. I remember going to bed that night and I'm sure I must have had a smile on my face thinking about what had happened during the day, and that was my introduction to Epping Forest.

Verderer Eric Dormer recalls childhood visits to a Retreat at Theydon Bois as a member of the Plaistow Primitive Methodist Chapel Sunday School and the wonderful teas they were given:

One eventually went up for huge wodges of bread and jam and vast cups of tea poured out of giant tea pots. The food was plain ordinary but large in volume and very acceptable to kids who'd been rushing around the Forest all day long. There were amusements there, sliding the mat, swings, donkey rides and all the rest of it, and our Sunday School teachers would also arrange races and competitions, but, and this is one of the things I'm glad I lived in the area when I did, the boys and the girls just went off into the Forest of their own free will, rather than having to be chaperoned in view of "the great dangers of the Forest".

There was a yearly visit to the Forest, usually to Theydon Bois but occasionally to Honey Lane and High Beach. These visits to which I refer were pre-war. Mostly our trips to Theydon Bois were made by train from Stratford but my earliest memory, when I was aged six or seven, was by horse brake. The thing I chiefly remember about this was on the lovely Saturday evening coming back up Buckhurst Hill, one of the lead horses fell over, lay on its side and refused to get up. One of our Sunday School teachers was a school master, but was the son of a Norfolk farmer, and he took some water, poured it in the horse's ear, and it got up. I've treasured this piece of information ever since, but I've yet to come across a horse lying on its side, refusing to get up and me in the possession of water!

Peter Fitch grew up in Chingford during the 1940s, his father was a milkman:

The helter-skelter at Jubilee Retreat, c1940s.

One of his customers was Mr Butler of Butler's Retreat, I'm also reasonably sure that he also took milk to the Jubilee Retreat, which sort of haunted me because there was this boarded up helter-skelter which just sat there waiting for the war to end. Of course it never did reopen; it was eventually taken away and, like all retreats in Epping Forest except Butler's Retreat, it never ever opened again. It was one of the few helter-skelters I'd seen in my life and it was all boarded up, what a shame for a 10 year old boy!

Mr Butler was not my father's favourite customer as I think he was a bit morose and short-tempered. I met him in about 1945 and he was a bit surly, it made you wonder what you'd gone there for; he wasn't the ideal retailer. But he kept it going, he never opened up any of the interior bit for the general public, but I gather that quite a large part of his trade was hiring out the inner room and another over it to Sunday school outings and things like that. He sold refreshments, oddly enough out of the same side-hatch that is still used today. It survived the war, just, as a V2 bomb landed absolutely on the edge of the pond which is less than 50 yards from it.

Chapter 9 – Managing the Forest

John Besent was Superintendent of Epping Forest from 1978 until 2001. He saw the Forest through a period of major road development, Dutch elm disease, BSE (so-called 'mad cow disease') and the decline of grazing, as well as instigating some radical changes to Forest management:

I was born in a North London suburb on the Northern Line, a place called Totteridge and went to school in Mill Hill which was not very far away either, so North London was my early home. I was always, as a boy, interested in trees if only in which to build dens and to get a viewpoint from which to watch cricket. I came across here on my bicycle never thinking that one day I would actually work here – extraordinary! This opportunity here came up out of the blue. I had never thought about coming here as there's only one job of this kind and that's here, so, you never really have an ambition to come to manage Epping Forest. Anyway, I got an interview for the post of Superintendent, and to my surprise I got the job.

I think the first thing that hit my wife and me was the public relations role that we were required to play. We had no understanding of this at all. It seemed to me when I first came here that this was a large tract of land with a lot of trees on it and the public had access to it and it needed to be managed. It never really occurred to me, perhaps it ought to have done, that there was going to be a substantial public relations role. It very quickly became clear that we were actually regarded as VIPs! We were invited to civic dos and I was asked to make presentations at speech days and all this kind of thing. I used to give lots of talks to people at various groups and even got invited to the university at Brighton to talk about Epping Forest. It was really quite extraordinary. This was something completely new to us, certainly to me. It did require us, having two young children, to spend a fortune on babysitters! But it was another aspect of the job which I enjoyed a great deal and I think that, to an extent, my wife did too. Sometimes we were invited to functions at Guildhall, state banquets and things of that kind. That was a huge privilege.

My first impressions of the Forest? Well, just so many trees quite frankly, unbelievable. Living at The Warren here, wherever one looked all one could see was trees! What I noticed most of all when I first drove around the front of the house and pulled up, it was dusk I think, were the rabbits; I'd never seen so many rabbits in my life! It was unbelievable, a sea of rabbits and I thought that The Warren was an aptly named place. Really, I think it was the treescape - it was solid woodland as far as the eye could see and it had a natural feel about it. Instantly you knew this wasn't a Forestry Commission plantation.

As far as the organisation was concerned it didn't come as a surprise to me really as I knew of the City of London and I knew of my predecessor and it was a traditional land agent's job, a resident land agent's job with a benign owner. Rather an old fashioned owner, but honest and doing a good job and that was how things seemed to me. My job was to carry out the instructions of my masters and they happened to be a committee, but they felt like owners. They didn't feel like absentee owners; they felt as if they were really interested, which they were. They were dedicated to Epping Forest.

Building up a management team here has been a huge change. In 1978, basically a one man band assisted by two or three people in the office, through to a management team. The current Superintendent, he's not a land agent; he's the chief executive directing the management team. We've now got the expertise to do the job of managing the Forest better than ever before.

I think a major change took place early on in my time. Hitherto, the Conservators had a preoccupation with the natural aspect as they took it to mean and they understood it to mean slowly guiding the Forest towards an uneven-aged high forest. That had really been the policy of the Conservators since 1878. They felt that was what people thought a forest ought to be like: single stemmed trees, uneven-aged woodland and lots of natural regeneration. Also, the Forest was managed essentially as woodland. Now, I just felt that was not really how it should be and I wondered why there was this pre-occupation with the natural aspect, as the Conservators understood it to be. Nobody ever made any mention of the Conservators' unqualified duty to conserve the Forest in all its vegetative forms. Preserving the natural aspect is something the Conservators are required to do to the extent that is possible, but conserving the Forest in all its vegetative forms, you know the pollards, the trees, the underwood, the heather, the herbage, conserving these things is an unqualified

John Besent (right) with his successor, Jeremy Wisenfeld, in 2001

duty, something the Conservators have to do. It was really never mentioned. I thought that was strange, so slowly I tried to influence the Conservators, to persuade them that they should be thinking of the Forest not just as a wooded area, but as an area which also comprised a substantial amount of open ground, (about a third of the Forest is roughly open ground) and that the open spaces of the Forest needed as much management as the woodland. Indeed they would often require more management because, by and large, the trees will look after themselves, but the open areas certainly won't.

Another fundamental change was the re-introduction of pollarding and the realisation that the natural aspect doesn't mean providing the sort of forest which the public expect to see or leaving nature to go her own way. It means the Forest has to appear to be natural; after all it's the natural <u>aspect</u> that has to be maintained as far as possible, not the natural being or the natural state. I think the Forest has to appear to be a natural place and, by and large, I think its visitors do feel that this is a seemingly natural place, managed in such a way that a broad range of vegetation types are conserved. I believe that effecting this change has been of fundamental importance.

It wasn't especially hard to convince the Committee to change, because all the while, you see, knowledge of ancient semi-natural woodland management amongst the scientific community was improving and that was rubbing off onto lay people, and members of the Committee were beginning to share in this improved knowledge. So they were able to understand where things had been going wrong in the past. A change of emphasis took place; it wasn't a change of direction. Some would say it was no more than a touch on the tiller, but it was an important change: a change to whole-forest management as opposed to the management of the Forest primarily as woodland.

I suggested to the Conservators in about 1990 that the time had come for us to have a written management plan. I wasn't suggesting that their management of the Forest in the past had been wrong. It had been undertaken given the knowledge that the Conservators had at that time, but the new management that they had embarked upon during the 1980's had really become quite complex. We needed to stop and say: where are we going? Let's find out what we've got, assess what we've got and prioritise areas for work.

The Committee were quite happy with this suggestion and I wanted them to have ownership of the plan from the word go, so we set up a steering group which comprised members of the Committee. It was really a sub-committee. It also contained representatives of English Nature and other external bodies as well, and the chairman of the working party, who was my deputy. I was a member of the steering group, too: and that group guided the work of the working party over a period of 3 or 4 years and more, right up to and including the plan production stage. All the while the plan was receiving the approval of the steering group, so when it actually came to presenting the finished plan to the Epping Forest Committee they accepted it completely.

The Superintendent and his staff are overseen by the Epping Forest and Open Spaces Committee which has had several name changes in its time and, no doubt, will have more in the future. Its aim though is essentially unchanged – to oversee the management of the Forest in the best interests of local people, visitors and the Forest itself. Its members represent the "Conservators of Epping Forest", the Corporation of London. It comprises two Aldermen of the City of London, 10 Members of the Corporation of London's Court of Common Council elected by the City and four Verderers, local people elected every seven years by Epping Forest Commoners, people who own or rent at least $^1/_2$ an acre of unencumbered land in a Forest parish. John Harvey was a Verderer from 1970 to 1998:

The Verderers used to meet at the Epping Forest Committee meetings which were monthly at Guildhall for nine months of the year, and the Verderers used to meet locally as much as was needed to discuss and visit areas that needed attention. For instance we would always look at road problems, at access problems through the Forest. All that sort of work that had to be done to satisfy ourselves that the right policies were being pursued by the Corporation. Our prime objectives being, at all times, of course, to protect the Forest from any form of encroachment and to uphold the Epping Forest Act.

Of course the result was that the local people and authorities came to look upon the Verderers as the mean of airing their views and representing their views to the Corporation. This kept us very busy and provided an enormous amount of correspondence, which leads me to add incidentally that the office of Verderer carried no financial reward and no compensation in respect of expenses that were incurred over the years. It really was an office undertaken by people who loved the Forest for the good of the Forest, in the best interest of the local population.

Dr. Eric Dormer recounts how he became a Verderer:

If one of the existing four Verderers either resigns and retires or dies while in office, then the 1878 Act of Parliament says that the Corporation of London shall appoint a Verderer until such time as the next septennial election comes along. And I had the great good fortune of appearing before the sub-committee of the Epping Forest Committee in 1981 to be interviewed and as a consequence of this was appointed Verderer.

The Chairman at that time, John Yates, had an unusual manner of address, his first words to me were "How many summers do you have?", which I soon realised meant how old was I. He was noted for wearing a camellia in his buttonhole. Subsequently, after his death, an area of land coming into the Forest was named Yates' Meadow in the honour of his chairmanship. When I appeared before that Committee, I expected to be asked perhaps about my interest in sectional activities in the Forest. In the Epping Forest Act, certain sections of the Forest can be set aside for such purposes as cricket, golf etc and I imagined that the Committee might not want somebody who was, for example, too mad keen a golfer. But I was a little surprised when one member of the Committee committed a Freudian mistake and said to me, "Well Doctor Dormer, I would be interested to know, have you been associated with any sexual activity in the Forest? Indeed, to open the question more broadly, what is your attitude to sexual activity in the Forest?" I obviously satisfactorily answered that question as I was subsequently appointed.

The regular workings of a committee are the same the world over, but the Epping Forest Committee has over 125 years of history and its own traditions that make it very unique. Dr Dormer explains the format of the regular Committee visits to the Forest:

The Committee visits the Forest on four Saturdays a year, to look at problems, to ensure that the Committee knows, at first-hand, areas of the Forest and of course for the Superintendent to show off what a good boy he has been in looking after the Forest. These visits are quite important, because for some years now no member of the Court of Common Council, ten of them sit on the Epping Forest and Open Spaces Committee, have lived in a Forest Parish and thus the four Verderers who by Act of Parliament must live in a Forest Parish, become very important

Originally, when I was on the Committee we carried on the coach which drove us around the Forest a member of the Town Clerk's Department and the committee secretary, and the problems were debated in the coach and the decision there made. But, of course, with the passing of the Freedom of Information Act this can no longer take place and so the committee now looks at the problems and then debates them at the Monday morning meeting at Guildhall of the full Committee. I must say that in my early days on the Committee, there was a tendency just for the Committee to get outside the coach and look, and sometimes only look through the windows! But, as the years have gone by the role of the Superintendent has been to lead his Committee walking through the Forest to ensure they really do know it on the spot, and this the Committee applauds.

All the fresh air of the Forest means that by lunchtime the Committee's appetites are sharpened and lunch is always very welcome. John Besent, former Superintendent of Epping Forest, picks up the story:

The lunches were really quite extraordinary affairs as they were out in the Forest. We used a tractor and trailer, which would be would be driven to some quiet spot in the Forest. The trailer might have been used for carting muck the day before, but it would have been washed down. A horse blanket was spread over the trailer and a linen tablecloth was laid over that. Then all the wines and spirits would be laid out with pork pies, sandwiches, fruit cake and cheese.

Fruit cake served with cheese is a Committee tradition. Dr. Dormer remembers one encounter with the Committee lunch before he was elected as a Verderer:

I was walking with my dog and came across a trailer in one the forest glades being laid out with food and drink I knew this was for the visiting committee who had not yet arrived, but just for fun I put my hand in my pocket chinked some coins and went up to one of the keepers and said "I'll have a Vermouth, if you please". He drew himself to attention, "Terribly sorry sir, not available to the general public!"

Another annual event is the Venison Supper; John Besent again:

The Venison Supper? Well, that really started life not as a venison supper but simply as a supper at the Temple in honour of the Playing Fields Committee. In October the Committee would, as part of their Saturday October meeting, visit the playing fields. They would meet the Playing Fields Committee and then entertain them to supper at the Temple. It may well have been venison, but at other times it may have been lamb, but it was always cooked by the Forest Keeper and his wife who lived next door. But in due time, certainly by my arrival we moved away from having the supper tagged onto a Saturday meeting. When you think about it, the Committee would have had lunch in the Garden House, then there might have been tea at The Warren and then they went down to the Temple for yet more food!

So it was moved away from the October Saturday meeting and became an event in its own right, usually later in the year, but it was still in honour of the Playing Fields Committee. All the members were invited. The chairman of the Playing Fields Committee was the chief guest. There were no other guests and more often than not we had venison. In fact eventually we always had venison; I would marinade it. One year it looked as if we wouldn't have anyone to cook the venison. I was quite happy to do it but in the event that was not necessary. The Superintendent had to be ready to do more or less anything! The supper was always an event to look forward to. It had to be experienced to be appreciated. The Conservators and their senior staff enjoyed themselves in the surroundings of the Temple and it all helped the esprit de corps.

However, not every Committee visit was a sylvan idyll. John Besent remembers taking a sub-committee to the Stump Road in the Epping part of the Forest to look at damage caused by horse riders, it was so muddy that:

I said you must take your wellington boots with you. The Chairman of the day was a chap called Harry Duckworth, a very nice man. He'd chaired all the important committees of the Corporation, but the Forest was completely strange to him. We set off along the Stump Road and it wasn't long before the Chairman got thoroughly stuck in the mud. The suction was so great that he couldn't actually get his boot out, so we had to lift him out of his wellington boots. The problem was that we dropped him! So we had to carry him out, and he came back to The Warren here and came into the house to use the bath!

The Forest Keepers are "the eyes and ears of the Conservators of Epping Forest". Jim Tilley was a Forest Keeper from 1964 to 1992. In his day, many Keepers worked both as a woodsman and a Keeper, and saw many changes:

Just prior to my starting as a Keeper, the Keepers had been on really a 24-hour stint. They lived in lodges on their areas and they could more or less work their times over the 24- hours. Everything that went on in that area they were responsible for. They weren't big areas, but enough for us to know what was going on there. We had to report any work that needed doing, like falling trees or blocked ditches or what have you. I patrolled Monk Wood and High Beach and I lived at Goldings Hill and Baldwins Hill. When I retired I lived at Goldings Hill, a nice old Tudor-style Lodge. It was very nice, very pleasant place. Then it was only foot patrol, walking. Then they introduced the two stroke motor cycle. You know there were quite a few mishaps on that as we weren't used to it! The Keepers now, the younger chaps, they're sort of brought up with powerful motor cycles, but in those days we had one or two funny instances with them, falling off and what have you. They weren't powerful bikes, we used to call them 'Noddy bikes', actually. It did get you there quicker, but now I don't think there's enough foot patrol now, it's not patrolled enough –

you see more when you're on foot. In Superintendent Qvist's time no little infringement was overlooked. If someone's garden fence bordered the Forest and if they put new fence up and it was about a foot out it was noted and they had to conform with it. They even had the surveyors there. Or some of the villages, the greens some of them would plant daffodils and that wasn't right, we had to go and dig them up.

Fred Fenson and Keith Bradley in 1980, the days before strict health and safety regulations!

Over the years the way in which the Forest was looked after changed:

All the likes of fencing, digging a hole to put a post in, all that's done by machinery now. When I came here they used to use cross cuts, you know cross cut saws but now they use power saws. We used to have massive bonfires, you'd say the fires were about 30 foot across. We used to burn the pollard stumps, you know on the pollard trees, the big stumps on the bottom. They could be having anything four or five foot down so we used to have massive fires and they would go for days on end, but all that finished because of the pollution law, the Clean Air Act. That didn't go down too well with the workers because we thought that leaving the brush there after that was a hazard. It could be once the stuff had dried out. The place didn't look so clean, not so neat and tidy. Sometimes we used to have these big fires and sometimes we'd be at one area for months. Take the Waterworks Corner we were there a long time, clearing the Forest there, just to allow the motorway to go through and that was quite a big job there. A lot of the people sort of thought we were devastating the Forest, the motorway objectors and all those people around and they didn't think much of it. A lot of them put it down to the Forest management, which it wasn't, it was the Ministry of Transport who had divine right sort of thing, but sometimes it was the chaps working who had the ear bashing, you know!

When I first started we had a very small staff, an office staff of about three and outside management. One chap used to do the golf courses and all the Forest management and then you had the Superintendent and now there are lots and lots! That's a sign of the times I suppose. I think it was a pleasure doing both sides, the maintenance side and the keepering side. You met so many different, interesting people and you got to know them over the years and had some good times with them, we used to meet up socially a lot with the chaps after work and some good times were had. It was a good place to work, we were treated well, yes the conditions were very good for working, That's how they hung onto the staff there, you know everyone seemed happy at their work, it wasn't a big turnover of labour there.

Graham Rawlings was a Forest Keeper from 1976 to 2000. His father Joe had also been a Keeper and indeed even lived in the same lodge on Mill Plain. He remembers the start of a typical day:

You'd invariably radio in from your lodge, you never had to go to any specific place to register and then you'd decide where you would be most needed on the patch of Forest you patrolled. I covered from Mill Plain right up to Buckhurst Hill, Knighton Wood and then from Mill Plain right down to Snaresbrook Road, this was all on foot.

You might be checking on wayleaves at the back of properties or making sure that no one had been chucking out rubbish and garden stuff over the back of the fence, which was always a problem. Walking around the perimeter and checking invariably took two or three days to do the complete area. Wayleaves are accesses that houses have over Forest land, they have to pay so much a year to have a garden gate to enter onto the Forest. It was always a case of people dumping stuff out of the garden, hedge trimmings and so on. If you found anything like that you had to go round to the front of the house and explain to the resident that the Forest is not a dumping ground and to pick it up and remove it. They always denied that it had come from their garden and they used to be very crafty sometimes. I remember on one occasion I walked round the back of a garden and there was a massive pile of grass and it was quite a high fence and I'd been to the front of this house several times but never found anyone in. I thought, "I know, I'll get my own back". So I found two pieces of wood and I virtually picked it all up and threw it back over the fence. It wasn't until several days later that I was told by one of my supervising officers to go round to this house and have a look and when I went round there, the gentleman had an all concrete back garden! Somebody from up the road had brought their rubbish round and dumped it outside his house, so I had to tidy his garden up.

Forest Keepers sometimes have to deal with dangerous situations; Graham remembers just one of them:

One particular keeper, Brian Gotts, had come across somebody in the St John's Ambulance Hut near the Bulrush Pond, it wasn't being used by St John's Ambulance, because it was unsafe. They'd forced the lock and were living in there, and Brian found them in there. He got threatened with a knife and radioed for assistance and, seeing as I was quite near, I joined him and we were both threatened, one chap waving a knife, the other waving a hammer. We decided to step back and let them go, but it was one of the things that was always in your mind, that you could end up getting really hurt. That is why I think now the Corporation do so much for personal safety, the Forest Keepers are out on their own and lives are threatened. I'm glad I'm not a Forest Keeper anymore; I don't think I could handle it.

Chapter 10 - Agriculture

The Davies family, Edgar (Eddie), Michael and now Andrew, have been farming the Epping Forest area for almost ninety years. They own of the last few working farms in the area. Verderer Michael Davies:

I can go back to when my father first started farming in Sewardstone and he took the tenancy of Sewardstone Hall on just before the First World War, at that time all the farm land that he was responsible for was down to grass. He had no livestock and the business at that time was cutting the grass for hay. This was done on a yearly basis and some particular years when there was plenty of growth, the grass may have been cut even twice in the same season.

This hay was then sold into London, by and large, to feed the stables that were quite significant in transport in central London at that time. So my father's business was really more to do with haymaking and feeding horses in London than perhaps producing food for humans, which you normally associate with agriculture today.

After the First World War things began to change. There weren't so many stables in London, motors were taking over from horse transport, but I can just remember in the 1930s when we still had horses and wagons carting hay into London, and we employed an outside contractor who would come and cut the hay and tie it in trusses to be loaded into wagons to go into London. Then the same wagons brought horse manure back from the stables to supply the growing Lea Valley glasshouses at the time, so it was a revolving process. Also in the 1920s and '30s my father introduced livestock onto the farm. We had some sheep but it was mainly dairy cattle at that time, supplying local dairies and I can remember our milk being taken to Soper's Dairy in Chingford.

At the time there was a lot of disease in dairy cattle, particularly bovine tuberculosis and we were at pains to eradicate the disease from our cattle, and this is when I perhaps first became conscious of the relationship between farming and the Forest. It was a great problem to separate our cattle from cattle that were grazing on the Forest which were not tested and free of TB at the time. We had to double fence all the fields that were near the Forest so that the cattle didn't get near one another, and it became quite obvious that we had to take quite dramatic measures to completely separate Forest cattle from our dairy cattle.

This developed as a conflict really, between local farming and the Forest. Subsequently, in the time of the Second World War when there was pressure to increase food production, and land was being ploughed up for production of arable crops, we again took the opportunity to separate the Forest from our dairy cattle by ploughing the fields adjacent to the Forest, and sowing them with wheat and barley principally. The reason for this was that it gave a better separation between our stock and other cattle in the Forest. From this we found another problem that our spring sown crops thrived quite well but our winter sown crops did very badly. And at the time we were not aware of what was the cause. Crops although they grew initially quite strongly, became stunted in the early summer time and then suffered from fungus and diseases. We now know of course, subsequently, that what we were suffering from was a virus disease; which was carried by greenfly, aphids that were living in the rough grass in the Forest. Nowadays of course we can cope with that by using aphicides. I illustrate this just to point out that over that period there was a conflict between farming adjacent to the Forest and the problems that arose.

I was not exercising the common rights that I had to graze in the Forest, because of the conflict that I was referring to between agriculture at that time and commoners grazing cattle. But going back to the 1930s the principal number of cattle in the Forest were in the hands of local small farmers who were principally dairy farmers producing milk for local consumption. There are one or two that I can remember – Mr Bird of Carroll's Farm, whose cows used to, in the summer period, graze on Sewardstone Green along the Bury Road and out onto Chingford Plain, and they would go back and forth every day. Sewardstone Green was a green then, it was open grass; it's not anymore. The Bury Road was open grass on both sides, it's not any more, and Chingford Plain was kept open by his cattle. This system worked extremely well because Mr Bird would keep his cows at home at night on his local field and they only went out after milking in the morning and came back from milking in the late afternoon. Consequently they were regularly supervised and rarely got into trouble or interfered with by other people.

Another farmer was Alec Roddick at Picks Farm, Sewardstone, who had a milk round and retailed his own milk in Sewardstone and Chingford area. His cows went onto Yardley Hill principally for grazing and kept to that area, Yardley Hill to Pole Hill. Alec's brother Frank Roddick of Springfield Farm on Lippitts Hill had a milk round around High Beach and down into Loughton. And he was the last man I can remember delivering his milk in a churn. He used to dip it out, and people came out with their jugs!

At that time the problems of commoners grazing animals was minimal because they were largely small dairy herds, where they were managed on a day-to-day basis and didn't have the opportunity, or very occasionally, to get where they shouldn't be. The Second World War changed all that. The pressure for maximum food production encouraged other people to come in who weren't the same sort of farmers as I've been referring to, who acquired small pieces of land in the area to enable them to register a right of common. They put animals on the Forest in considerable numbers as there was no restriction on numbers at that time, and the numbers of cattle went up to 200-300 on the Forest.

This was a different type of use of the common right, it was more a ranching type of use than a closely managed use. They were turned out and left to their own devices for long periods and not closely managed and they tended to move towards the south, towards Wanstead as that's where the best grazing was. Although the animals might be turned out in the Waltham Abbey area or High Beach area, it wasn't long before they all moved down to Wanstead. From that time there was increasing pressure on the Conservators to do something about the problem of animals getting into people's gardens, getting on the highway and causing all sorts of problems.

It was a conflict between the development of a different social structure in the Forest area which had gone on before, this came to a head in the early 1960s and the Conservators made up their minds they'd got to do something about it. The Verderers of the time had several meetings with the commoners to try to resolve the situation. Ideas were put forward like tethering cattle and what have you which wasn't very practical, but the final outcome was that the right of common grazing was prohibited in the winter period from November to April, as it was felt that there wasn't much for them to eat in the Forest and they were probably causing more trouble by straying away from Forest land

Head Forest Keeper Paul Liquorish, Forest Keeper Joe Rawlings and Peter Adams (now a Verderer) in 1976.

during the winter period. The graziers were compensated for the loss of that right.

And from that time on, through the late '60s to the '80s, the number of cattle grazing on the Forest gradually diminished and became less and less, and in 1996 we were down to something less than ten animals grazing on the Forest. There was the outbreak of BSE which brought in the regulation that animals of more than thirty months of age could not go into the food chain and, of course, the type of grazing in the Forest would only fatten animals after more than 30 months. The tradition over the last 50 years had been to purchase what was called 'strong stores'. These would be animals of two to three years old that were not fat, turn them out in the spring and the animals of that age would put on weight and be fit for the butcher by the autumn. But of course they were more than 30 months of age, and that was the finish of commoner's cattle grazing in the Forest.

In 1998 the Conservators decided to reintroduce cattle grazing in the Forest (it had stopped in 1996 when no commoners turned their

cattle out) in an attempt to manage areas of grassland and heath land that otherwise would have disappeared. In 2002, in partnership with EW Davies Farms Ltd, a herd of magnificent English Longhorn cattle were turned out once again to graze the Forest during the summer months. Of course, cattle wandering free-range around the Forest has caused its fair share of problems. Brian Dyer recalls one such event:

There were lots of cattle around and I remember that I had driven up to the newly constructed Waterworks gyratory system and somebody had left the gate open and there was a whole herd of cattle in the middle of the road. There were these two young policemen who'd been sent from Hackney to clear the road, so I had to stop anyway so I said "Would you like me to get rid of them for you?". "Yes", they said, so I said, "Keep the gate open". I got hold of one and led it carefully through and it went and the others followed. Because having lived here all my life you knew how to deal with the cows and there was no problem with them. But you couldn't hurry them up and to hoot at them was disastrous as they'd run and bump into your car, especially round the Whipps Cross area, there were a lot there. They were hazardous and it was disastrous if they got down the road as they'd push the gates open and eat the hedges and flowers but I always felt that the people who wanted them banned, shouldn't have

Longhorn cattle in Epping Forest

moved here in the first place! They weren't hazardous, only when they went down George Lane. Shop-keepers would hurry out with pails of water to keep them happy and keep them out of the shops.

John Harvey as Member of Parliament for Walthamstow East from 1955 until 1966, remembers problems the cattle caused him:

Many of my constituents, I remember, used to complain about the wandering cattle who walked into their gardens uninvited and chewed daffodils and things like that. It was a bit difficult to try to explain to people that the cattle really did have priority over householders in the sense that the cattle had rights going back into the pages of history, whereas the householders concerned had developed the building they had lived in, in very recent years.

Chapter 11 – Protecting the Forest

As former Superintendent of Epping Forest, John Besent is in a unique position to comment on the increasing encroachment of urbanisation of the Forest:

The decision to go ahead with the M25 was pretty much made by the time I came here. It still had to go through the Parliamentary process, but the decision on the routing had been made. Getting the road to tunnel through the Forest at more or less its narrowest point had been a hard struggle for the Conservators, but it could have been even more difficult had it not been for the horrendous situation at Waterworks Corner. Everyone could see how ghastly that was. The situation at Waterworks Corner arose from the rerouting of the North Circular Road at Waltham Forest in the early 1970s as you drive down the A104 through Woodford Green you come to this enormous roundabout with a major road going underneath. Well that was Forest land. It's a huge cutting, an horrendous scar across the Forest. I think if that hadn't happened we would have had an even more difficult battle over the M25. We may not have got the tunnel at Epping under Mill Plain. Bell Common is further to the north. The tunnel should really be called the Mill Plain tunnel.

The first proposal was to have a surface route though the Forest in the Chingford area at its widest point. The Conservators persuaded the road planners that they had to go much further north at least. The ideal would have been beyond the Lower Forest, but the Committee had to settle for Mill Plain where the Forest was very narrow. The proposal there was for a surface road with an intersection with the A11 (now renumbered B1393). The Conservators weren't happy with that at all, so there was more opposition and the proposals were changed to allow a half length tunnel at Mill Plain. This was I believe the proposal which went to the public inquiry in 1975. The Conservators were bitterly opposed to a half length tunnel and to an interchange with the A11. They wanted a full length tunnel. The Friends of Epping Forest, who had been formed to fight the road, were very helpful in the support they gave the Conservators. Suffice to say that the inspector recommended in his report that the tunnel should become full length and there should be an interchange at Honey Lane. It was on this basis that the road went to Parliament, You see

Parliament had to give its authority for land to be taken from Epping Forest for the motorway. It was not appropriate for Forest land to be acquired under the Compulsory Purchase Acts. Exchange land was provided for in the settlement and as this covered Forest land which was only temporarily required for the duration of the works as well as land which would be permanently taken from the Forest, the Forest gained a few acres, but it was a hard fought battle.

The other scheme that I had on my plate, really from the day I arrived to the day I retired, was the Hackney / M11 link road and again we fought for the road to be in tunnel. There were two public inquiries: one was the line order public inquiry and the other was the compulsory purchase order inquiry which didn't really affect us as Forest land wasn't going to be compulsory acquired. Again Parliament would be asked to give its authority and again exchange land would be required.

The original proposal was to have a surface road across the Green Man with a one-way flyover, similar to the one at Gallows Corner on the Southend Arterial Road. It was going to be like that - awful, absolutely awful and there were going to be no facilities for people on foot or horseback to get from one side to the other. It was going to be terrible. What we have now after another long, hard-fought battle is the new road underground at both The Green Man and George Green. There are big underpasses for horses at The Green Man and a very wide bridge over the Central Line for horses and cattle. This has tall side walls. You don't have to get off your horse to go through the underpasses. Compare them with the nasty little underpass on the North Circular Road at Waltham Forest. That is just like a rat hole and people are supposed to go through there – terrible. At the Green Man interchange, there is now a physical connection between Leyton Flats and Bush Wood as the land within the new roundabout has been dedicated to the Forest, You can now get from one part of the Forest to the other. The Link Road tunnels were a long haul, but it's been worthwhile and the settlement that was approved by Parliament included 20 acres of exchange land, about three times the acreage that was permanently taken from the Forest for the road scheme. My role was to advise the Conservators, articulate their concerns to the road planners and to actually fight the case when it came to the public inquiry.

The M11 had a major influence on the Epping New Road and traffic did tail off

Road Development at Waterworks Corner

for a while. When I went to the Commons Select Committee hearing during the passage of the City of London (Various Powers) Bill in 1978, which was to allow the M25 to be built through Epping Forest, one of the experts for the Ministry said that with the M11 already in being and following the construction of the M25, the Epping New Road would revert to a quiet country by-way! Certainly, for a period of time, it was quieter. All the lorries went. Even now they form a very small proportion of the total number of vehicles on the Epping New Road, as they use the M11 instead. But the amount of commuter traffic has built and built and built. In addition to the normal 4% compound increase in traffic each year, there has been additional traffic generated by new housing developments and the M25, which has brought new commercial development in its wake.

It is now difficult and dangerous to cross the road. At one time if you went out from here with a horse at 8 o'clock in the morning during the rush hour you might find it difficult to cross the road, but now at any time of the day crossing the road on horseback can be very difficult and dangerous. The surprise is that more people and horses have not been killed or injured, but huge numbers of animals are killed on the Forest's busy roads each year.

John Harvey voices concerns that were current both in his time as a Verderer and today:

One of the main problems that still faces the Verderers and the Committee as a whole is, of course, the size of the Forest and the amount of land that could be used for housing if the Forest were left free. Fortunately there's been no change so far between the Corporation of London and the government over the use of Forest land. If you think about it the whole of Epping Forest from Leyton and Wanstead right across to Epping could by now have been turned into housing and have ceased to be the great attraction that it is to local residents. It is of course worth making a point that where land has been taken from the Forest, for example for road development (and of course Parliament can always threaten new legislation to remove the Corporation's powers over any particular aspect), we have managed to establish a position in which the authority in developing land is bound to acquire more land on the fringes of the Forest and thus we have managed to establish a situation where in fact there is more Forest land today than there was in 1870 when the Corporation of London took charge of the Forest.

The Corporation has also been buying Buffer Land on the edges of the Forest to protect the Forest itself, and by buying Buffer Land and making it part of the Forest structure, it is actively seeking to stop all sorts of development on the edges of the Forest, that will be essential to the survival of the Forest itself. The Corporation has spent a great deal of money in recent years buying Buffer Land in the interest of maintaining the Forest.

As the twentieth century advanced, new developments in housing and road building threatened the peaceful nature of Epping Forest. Pollution increased and the ecosystem was adversely affected. Buffer Land is primarily agricultural land on the northern fringes of the Forest held in perpetuity to protect the Forest. John Besent comments on how the policy came into being:

You've only got to look at the records and you can see how the Green Belt has dwindled over the decades, especially in the area of Waltham Abbey. One couldn't rely upon Green Belt designation to protect the rural environs of the Forest. Given time, more and more land was going to go, and the only way it seemed to me that one could protect this land was to have ownership of it, to buy it.

We were lucky with Woodredon and Warlies Park Estate. It wasn't due to come to us on the abolition of the Greater London Council, who had bought it under the Green Belt (London and Home Counties) Act 1930. It was due to go Essex County Council because it was in their administrative area. But, we thought that it should come to us to be managed in conjunction with the Forest, so we asked the Minister to give it to us and not to Essex. He saw the sense in this and agreed. It had been Forest land many centuries ago. It gets its name, I think, from a royal decree that it could be rid of wood. It was agreed that the estate should be managed not as Forest land but in sympathy with the Forest and for its protection. I suggested to the Conservators that in the interests of protecting more of the Forest, they should further pursue the Buffer Land policy and they agreed.

Chapter 12 - Wildlife

Technological advancements and social change in the twentieth century have threatened, but not destroyed, the flora and fauna of the Forest. For some people, the first time they visited the Forest was an eye opening experience. Allan Brafield was one such person:

I was born in India, a land of tropical and sub-tropical forests which I had come to love. I arrived in England in October 1948. I settled in Barkingside and was pleased to learn that there was a forest nearby. I promised myself an early visit and remember wondering what the wildlife might be like. Snakes? Possibly. Wild boar? Must wait and see.

The memory of that first visit will always remain with me. It was a clear, sunny autumn morning with a light breeze. I stopped my car somewhere near High Beach Church and alighted, to find myself standing in a shimmering golden forest, with here and there bright green and russet browns. I had never seen anything remotely like this before – I even walked on a carpet of gold! I was familiar with ferns; but golden ones? Had there been anyone with me at the time I would have been totally speechless, with no adjectives at my disposal to describe what I was seeing and feeling.

But, even for seasoned Forest visitors there are always new surprises. Verderer Eric Dormer remembers an event in the 1960s:

I'd often spoken to my wife about the kingfishers and said it was most easy to see them early in the morning. So, one rather lovely summer morning we got up about 6 o'clock and went and sat in our wellingtons, hidden inside a holly bush. In due course I remember a man walk past with his dog, and the look of amazement on his face at seeing two adults sitting side by side in their wellingtons in the middle of a holly bush!

Sadly, some species have declined or vanished over the last hundred years. Frank Gentry was a Boy Scout in the 1930s:

Our scoutmaster was keen that we improved our knowledge of natural history.

As we walked across Chingford Plain, skylarks were singing overhead, and once we found a nest with eggs. You'll be glad to know that we left it intact. In the Forest we heard woodpeckers drumming and cuckoos calling. Among the bushes flitted robins and chaffinches, and several times we saw grass snakes. Also, there were red squirrels and white admiral butterflies, sadly now both gone from the area. We were told all the names of the trees, including hornbeam, oak, beech and silver birch, with holly and hawthorn bushes.

Hornbeams, c 1970s

Hilda Anslow and her sister, Vera, have been regular visitors to the Forest for many years. Hilda remembers the deer:

At week-ends, we usually saw groups of deer. We would stop and they would look at us and then trot quietly away gradually disappearing into the undergrowth. On one occasion we were following one of our secret little paths, I think it was in the Great Monk Wood area, when we heard a funny clicking noise. We stopped and looked around and there to our surprise were two beautiful stags having a fight and the clicking noise was the clash of their antlers. When they got wind of us they broke apart and trotted away with their tongues lolling out: not more than five or six foot away. We have never been so close to a stag before or since.

Another time we were in the same area on a little path which was only wide enough for one person and I was in the lead when I was startled by a terrific bellow and standing in front of me was a magnificent stag with a lovely set of antlers. I stared in disbelief and as it was obvious he wasn't going to give ground, I decided discretion was the better part of valour and backed away, leaving him lord of his harem. Actually I didn't see the hinds as there was a lot of shrubby growth around but assumed I had accidentally stumbled into his territory. We spent many happy hours horse riding in the Forest in the 1950s and one of the best ways to see the deer was from the back of a horse. You could get quite close to them as they had no fear of horse legs. We were very sad when the deer were moved to the sanctuary, as to us they were so much a part of the Forest, but it is in the best interests of the deer.

Not all the deer are in the sanctuary, some can still be glimpsed in the northern Forest. Former Forest Keeper Jim Tilley says that a sighting ...

...depends on if there are dogs around, but sometimes you can be walking in an area and you might come across four or five, just grazing. There are deer in the Forest but I think they are mostly in the Copped Hall area, as that's a big estate. They sometimes venture into the Forest themselves when they get a scent of the deer sanctuary. There's anything up to 140 in there, so that might attract them to that area, but there's nothing in seeing around the Wake Arms a herd of about $^1/_2$ a dozen there, just at certain times of the year. That part coming down from the Wakes Arms towards Loughton that would be on your right, towards the apex of the A11 and the Loughton road, that's called Deershelter Plain and that used to have sort of shelters there for the deer and they used to feed them there and that's why they called it Deershelter. So perhaps it's instinct that keeps them there, I don't know.

Over the last century red squirrels have vanished from the Forest. Jim Tilley says that amongst the other species that have dwindled are hares:

When I first came on the Forest we used to see a lot of hares but now you never see a hare. Especially at certain times of the year you know they are 'as mad as a March hare' and they used to box each other and play around, and on one or two areas there seemed to be quite a few of them. But now, in the latter years I never saw one, but people taking dogs out might have frightened them away from those areas. It was the same with the badgers. There were one or two places noted for badger setts but over the years, they've more or less gone out of the Forest, they might be on the borders of the Forest one or two places. They like fields and forest.

Fallow does

The number of wildflowers has also declined, as Barbara Morris remembers from her walks from Whitehall Road to Chingford Plain:

Well, you don't see many flowers in the Forest, now. You don't see as many cowslips and lovely violets as we used to get. As you're going down and then up the hill, there's the Forest on both sides, we used to get the violets there, but there are no violets there, they're all gone. But on the left as you're going down the hill from Japanese Woods you go down the slope and go to the top of the hill where the golfers go from, on the right, the Forest is a bit thicker there; you get some lovely dog roses and that's really full of dog roses. It's so pretty but we're losing a bit more and more, why I don't know but there were more flowers when I was young.

Many regular Forest users feel that there are now far more people using the Forest, especially dog walkers and this has had a detrimental effect on the Forest's animals. Naturalist Ken Hoy says:

I used to take a group through the Forest, on a Sunday or a Saturday and hardly see anyone at all and you'd see groups of deer but there is a major difference now, of course, in that any part of the Forest you come upon somebody or other and a dog every five or six hundred yards. I think that might be one of the causes of the badgers leaving and the deer casualties; certainly we see more people going deeper into the Forest and I think that change came about when car ownership increased and the car parks in the northern part of the Forest were introduced.

But in my youth the far northern parts of the Forest, far from where I was living in Woodford, were quite desolate spots where you hardly ever saw anyone. In the summer we had family picnics and we used to go to the' other forest', as we called it and I remember the tall bracken and this was a big change, we're talking about when I was 6,7 or 8 at the most. One of the memories I have is of being on Deershelter Plain, playing hide and seek when the bracken was high in the August holidays. I was crawling underneath, I was hiding from my sister and my father and so on, and I came out, crept out onto a path and I remember looking down and seeing a baby deer down the path and it was looking at me. I assumed it was just a baby deer, but it had little antlers, little prick antlers with a couple of spikes on them, and it was only years and years later that I realised that that could have been a roe deer, and, of course, the date couldn't have been earlier than 1929 and no later than '31, so whether it was one of the roe which were supposed to have disappeared about 1920 or not, it's a possibility. I have this very clear picture of this little baby deer with little spiky antlers.

Chapter 13 – And finally...

Many of the people quoted in this book have noticed changes to the Forest throughout the 20th century - some changes for the better, some for the worse. What they all agree on, however, is that Epping Forest is a fantastic resource and one that they hope new generations will enjoy just as much as they have.

Mary Ashbridge-Taylor:

With the end of the 1930s and the Second World War came the beginning of great changes to the Forest. Motor vehicles, road building, increased population and development of all kinds brought an end to the old way of life. Maybe we were the unintentional vandals of the day, but we really loved the Forest, and thanks to Forest management, better education, and fierce protection of the land, it is still there offering enjoyment and freedom to every one of us, we hope for many years to come.

Hilda Anslow:

Have there been many changes since 1937? I think there have, but these come slowly and sometimes imperceptibly. There were no car parks in those days; there were so few cars, there was no need for them. One of the beauties of the Forest was that it was so peaceful and quiet that we saw things that we could not hope to see now. Whether tractors were used in the maintenance of the Forest pre-war we're not sure, but we remember when lovely shire horses pulled the felled trees out on wooden sledges. They were much kinder to the Forest and fitted in naturally with their surroundings. We today (early November) passed a gang of workmen removing felled trees with a grabber and lorry, churning up the forest floor. Give me the gentle giants any day. There seems to be a lot more dead and dying trees now. The small paths we used to use are no longer there perhaps because we do not walk them regularly now, and the wider paths have become rather artificial horse rides. There are a lot more people using the interior of the Forest, whether on foot, horseback or bicycles. But in spite of this it is still possible to do a 20 mile figure-of-eight walk in the Forest, with very little road walking, only crossing the roads, and rarely meeting any people. On a Saturday morning in November we walked from The Roebuck to the Information Centre at High Beach (about three miles) and saw three people, one a man exercising his dogs, a jogger and a biker, who yelled at us to get out of his way.

Sylvia Mason:
I married in 1965 we then had a car. The three children came along. We had a caravanette, and most Sundays we took the children to the Forest and had ice creams or meat pies from the Retreat, and watched the 'planes or kites. Now my three grandsons love the Forest, to climb on the cut down old trees and it's a 'must'- hot chocolate, chips or ice cream at the Retreat, when they come to visit me in Chingford.

Stan Gailer:
I still use the Forest, as I now live in Highams Park. We go up the back of the lake and there's a big green round the back of the lake which is very nice. Every morning you probably find about 3, 4 even 8 dogs all with their owners and we all know each other, so we know which dog's going to fight, which dog's not going to fight. But its lovely up there, in the morning at about half past eight. Sometimes, we go through the Forest and come home through the Forest, which is even better. Otherwise, you know I'm getting on now and I drive up now, it's lazy but I usually walk through the woods by myself. So, it's lovely!

Ken Hoy:
There are differences, currently, about the extent to which the Conservators might enthusiastically wish to recreate what is being called the "pasture" or pasture woodland. I'm not against that and I don't think many of the Friends are. There was some concern about fences and enclosures but that has sort of gone past now, to some extent. However, there is concern about the extent to which they want to re-pollard. I accept that it is great to have re-pollarding as a form of management to let the sunlight in, but to designate a lot of the Forest, where there might happen to be a pollard tree, just to call it wood pasture, and then to manage it so that it once again becomes what might be called medieval wood pasture is, I think, spurious. And that's what we're concerned about whether that is the intention or not of the management.

Harry Berry:
I remember one particular thing, it always used to amaze me. We used to have to go to Epping regularly and in those days the stretch between the Wake Arms

At High Beach in the 1950s.

and the Robin Hood had overhanging trees and it was like going through a tunnel, and when they cut down those trees it spoilt the whole character of that area; it was so different as you came down the road into this tunnel of trees. I don't know why they did it. I suppose they did it because of traffic and that.

Ivy Alexander:

When people mention Epping Forest I have a lot of memories of the reverence that the older generation had for the Forest because it meant a lot to them and going generations back, to my father's grandparents and their parents, they came from the Forest area and they got their living from the Forest. It was gradually encroached upon and bits taken, so that those that actually came from the Forest then didn't get a chance to go into the Forest, they were pushed out and finished up in places like my family in West Ham and Canning Town.

When we did go into the Forest for the day we were these scruffy children from the East End and people had to disinfect the Forest after we'd gone! [17] When actually, going back historically certainly my family came from Epping Forest and if it hadn't have been for the efforts of these people to save Epping Forest

---

[16] Reference to folklore which said that the streets of Loughton were washed down after East End children had visited Shaftesbury Retreat.

then it wouldn't be there now. I know why my family spoke with almost tears in their eyes of Epping Forest; now when I think of Epping Forest I'm practically the same. Epping Forest meant a lot to me and it still does.

John Besent, former Superintendent of Epping Forest:

Now, places I liked best in Epping Forest. I regard this place as heritage Britain in landscape terms and what appeals to me most about the Forest is that it's a haven of peace and tranquillity but at the same time it's a spiritually uplifting place. So, at the same time you get the peacefulness, and one chap who responded to the Quality of Life survey talked about somewhere you can go to think over a problem or get over a loss, and that's very true. You've got the tranquillity you've got the quietness and at the same time it's uplifting. I think the duality there also comes together in my mind at Loughton Camp. It's the most peaceful place well away from traffic, especially on a still November morning when there's no wind. You're seemingly miles away from anywhere, there's no traffic and yet you have total peace, and quiet and these wonderful cathedral-like trees reaching up to the sky. Uplifting.

For me, Loughton Camp actually says it all and other places pale into insignificance compared to Loughton Camp. I love Warren Hill, the open plateau of Warren Hill, an oasis so close to the office and the Epping New Road, it's an oasis almost up there! In the far south, Gilbert's Slade. Again if you switch off in your mind the traffic noise, that you can't see, you could be anywhere and yet you're so close to London in Gilbert's Slade, but it's got its bomb craters, which are ponds or gravel workings, its got pollarded trees, its got grass, virtually every type of vegetation is in Gilberts Slade and from the interior there, you can't see housing to the east and you can't see the road to the west and for me that's another gem, In fact the Forest is a gem, it's a cameo national park.